A LIFE
UNBURDENED

THE SWEDISH ART OF LETTING GO

Attia Zia

A Life Unburdened:
The Swedish Art of Letting Go

© 2024 Attia Zia
All Rights Reserved.

No part of this book may be reproduced or transmitted in any form or by any means, electronic or mechanical, including photocopying, recording, or any information storage and retrieval system, without prior written permission from the author, except for the use of brief quotations in a book review or scholarly journal.

Published by:
Treasured Print Design
Wheaton, IL, USA

Cover Design: Treasured Print Design
Edited by: Attia Zia

Disclaimer:
The information contained in this book is for informational purposes only and is not intended as a substitute for professional advice. The author and publisher shall not be liable for any damages or adverse consequences resulting from the use or application of any information or strategies discussed in this book.

Contents

PREFACE 1
INTRODUCTION 5

Chapter 1
THE GENTLE ART OF SWEDISH DEATH CLEANING 11

Chapter 2
MINDFULNESS AND THE DECLUTTERING PROCESS 21

Chapter 3
PRACTICAL STEPS FOR LETTING GO 33

Chapter 4
THE EMOTIONAL JOURNEY OF LETTING GO 47

Chapter 5
CREATING A SUPPORTIVE ENVIRONMENT FOR LETTING GO ... 61

Chapter 6
MAINTAINING A CLUTTER-FREE LIFESTYLE 75

Chapter 7
EMBRACING MINIMALISM AND INTENTIONAL LIVING 89

Chapter 8
THE IMPACT OF DECLUTTERING ON MENTAL HEALTH 103

Chapter 9
FOSTERING CONNECTIONS AND BUILDING
 MEANINGFUL RELATIONSHIPS 117

Chapter 10
CREATING A LEGACY OF INTENTIONAL LIVING 133

ABOUT THE AUTHOR 145

Preface

In a world where possessions often define our lives, it's easy to become overwhelmed by the sheer volume of things we accumulate. This book, **"A Life Unburdened - The Swedish Art of Letting Go,"** is a heartfelt guide to simplifying your life and rediscovering what truly matters.

My journey into the realm of decluttering began with a deeply personal experience: helping my 82-year-old mother clear out her studio and 20 years of belongings that had quietly taken over her life. The process was not just about removing physical items; it was a profound emotional journey that prompted reflections on memories, relationships, and the weight of the past. Watching her transition from a cluttered space to one that embraced simplicity was a testament to the transformative power of letting go.

As I navigated this experience with my mother, I realized that decluttering is a universal challenge that resonates with many. It is not solely about tidying up; it's about creating space for joy, connection, and purpose. This understanding led me to explore the principles of Swedish death cleaning—a mindful approach to decluttering that emphasizes the importance of letting go for the benefit of ourselves and our loved ones.

In this book, I will share practical strategies, personal anecdotes, and insights that I have gained through my own decluttering journey. You will find guidance on recognizing emotional attachments, establishing a supportive environment, and maintaining a clutter-free lifestyle. More importantly, I hope to inspire you to embrace the art of letting go and to understand that decluttering can lead to a life filled with intention and fulfillment.

Whether you are just beginning your journey or seeking to maintain a simplified life, I invite you to embark on this transformative process. Together, we can create spaces that reflect our true selves, nurture meaningful connections, and cultivate a legacy that honors what we hold dear.

Thank you for joining me on this path toward a lighter, more intentional life.

Warmly,
Attia Zia

Introduction

Welcome to **"A Life Unburdened: The Swedish Art of Letting Go."** This book is designed to guide you through the transformative process of decluttering your life by embracing the principles of Swedish death cleaning. By letting go of the excess—both physical and emotional—you can create space for what truly matters, allowing you to live a more intentional and fulfilling life.

In our fast-paced world, it's easy to accumulate possessions, memories, and emotional baggage that weigh us down. This book aims to help you release those burdens, offering practical strategies and emotional insights to assist you on your journey. Each chapter will guide you through understanding the philosophy behind Swedish death cleaning, navigating the emotional complexities of letting go, and implementing practical decluttering techniques.

To support your progress, you'll find useful tools, including the **"My Goals for This Week"** worksheet and a **Habit Tracker**. These resources are designed to help you set specific, achievable goals and cultivate positive habits that will sustain your decluttering journey.

Additionally, after each chapter, you'll find **journal pages** that encourage you to reflect on your experiences and insights. These pages will allow you to document your thoughts, track your progress, and personalize your journey toward a clutter-free life. Engaging with the journal prompts helps deepen your understanding of the material and creates a space for you to explore your feelings as you navigate the process of letting go.

My Goals for This Week

In the **"My Goals for This Week"** worksheet, you'll identify your primary goal for the week—whether it's decluttering a specific area of your home, establishing a new self-care routine, or initiating a personal project. By writing down your goal and outlining the actionable steps to reach it, you will create a clear path forward. Breaking your goal into manageable tasks helps you stay focused and motivated as you progress.

Habit Tracker

The **Habit Tracker** included in this book is designed to help you cultivate and maintain positive habits throughout the month. By tracking your daily habits, you can enhance your accountability and recognize your progress. Some suggested habits include:

- Daily decluttering for a few minutes.
- Practicing mindfulness or meditation.
- Engaging in physical activity.
- Reading inspirational material.
- Maintaining a gratitude journal.

Each day of the week is represented with checkboxes, allowing you to mark off completed habits. This visual representation of your progress will motivate you to stay consistent and committed to your goals.

Journal Pages

After each chapter, you'll find dedicated **journal pages** that encourage self-reflection and personal growth. These pages include prompts to help you process what you've learned and how it applies to your life. You can explore your thoughts, document your feelings, and outline your progress as you move through your decluttering journey.

Moving Forward

As you embark on this journey of decluttering and letting go, remember that progress is not always linear. Embrace the ups and downs as part of the process and be gentle with yourself along the way. By utilizing the **"My Goals for This Week"** worksheet, **Habit Tracker**, and **journal pages**, you will have the tools necessary to set meaningful goals and create lasting habits that support your journey to a clutter-free life.

Let's dive in and begin the transformative journey toward a life unburdened, where you can create the space for joy, connection, and what truly matters.

> # CHAPTER 1

The Gentle Art of Swedish Death Cleaning

Let's face it—most of us have too much stuff. Whether it's a drawer overflowing with mysterious cables for gadgets long forgotten or a closet packed with clothes that haven't seen the light of day in years, clutter seems to multiply when we're not looking. It can feel like our belongings are slowly overtaking our homes and lives.

But fear not! Enter the world of Swedish Death Cleaning—or, as the Swedes call it, döstädning. Before you start imagining dark rooms and somber music, let's clarify: Swedish death cleaning is not as morbid as it sounds. In fact, it's a liberating and often joyful process that helps you declutter your life and prioritize what truly matters.

In this chapter, we'll explore the philosophy behind Swedish death cleaning, how to get started, and how this gentle art can bring more joy and lightness to your life than you ever imagined.

What Is Swedish Death Cleaning, Anyway?

Let's start with the obvious: What exactly is Swedish death cleaning? Contrary to its name, this practice isn't about preparing for death in a gloomy way. Instead, it's a mindful approach to sorting through your belongings, deciding what's essential, and letting go of what no longer serves you. The goal is to lighten your physical and emotional load, making life easier for both you and your loved ones before they have to take on that responsibility.

This isn't about rushing to empty your house in a frantic weekend blitz. Swedish death cleaning is a slow, intentional process that encourages reflection on your belongings, your memories, and your legacy. The aim is to create a home that feels lighter, simpler, and more aligned with the life you want to live—now and in the future.

In short, it's a thoughtful way to tidy up, ensuring that your loved ones aren't overwhelmed by a mountain of items when you're gone. But this approach is not just for seniors or those planning their final farewell; it's for everyone, at any age, and it can transform how you live your life right now.

Why "Death" Cleaning?

Now, let's address the elephant in the room: why include "death" in the term? In Swedish, döstädning combines *dö* (death) and *städning* (cleaning), and the concept is straightforward. By organizing your life, you spare your family from the daunting task of sorting through your belongings after you're gone. The Swedish have a pragmatic approach to life and death, making this process a gift to those you care about.

However, Swedish death cleaning isn't solely about death; it's about living well. It focuses on freeing yourself from unnecessary items, ensuring you're surrounded by things that bring you joy and serve a purpose. Clearing the clutter opens up space for creativity, freedom, and a lighter, more fulfilling life.

How Is It Different from Regular Decluttering?

You might wonder, "Isn't this just another form of spring cleaning or minimalism?" Not quite. While Swedish death cleaning shares similarities with other decluttering methods, it adds a unique layer of intention. Unlike most trends that focus on tidying up for personal benefit, this approach emphasizes consideration for your loved ones.

When decluttering, think about what will happen to your belongings when you're no longer here. Will your family be burdened with sorting through sentimental items? By taking control now, you alleviate that responsibility and gain peace of mind.

The Benefits of Swedish Death Cleaning

So, why engage in Swedish death cleaning? Here are some benefits:

1. **Less Stuff, Less Stress:** A cluttered environment can overwhelm your senses and make it difficult to relax. Clearing out the mess creates a calmer space where you can recharge.
2. **A More Intentional Life:** This process compels you to reflect on your belongings and make conscious choices about what to keep, fostering a lifestyle where each item has a purpose.
3. **Freedom from Emotional Weight:** Physical belongings can carry emotional burdens. Letting go of items that no longer serve you can lighten your mental load, freeing you from guilt and nostalgia.
4. **A Gift to Your Loved Ones:** By decluttering now, you're sparing your family from having to tackle this task later. They can focus on celebrating your life and cherishing your memories.

Where to Begin: Taking the First Step

Now that you understand Swedish death cleaning, let's discuss how to get started. The thought of sorting through all your belongings may feel overwhelming, but you don't have to do it all at once. Start small.

1. **Begin with Easy Items:** Start with things that don't hold much emotional weight. Focus on areas like your kitchen or garage, where practical items can be easily identified and sorted.
2. **One Area at a Time:** Avoid trying to declutter everything at once. Focus on one small space—be it a drawer or shelf—and commit to completing that area before moving on.
3. **Be Kind to Yourself:** Decluttering can stir up emotions. As you sort through your belongings, it's normal to feel attached to certain items. Take your time, and acknowledge your feelings.
4. **Involve Your Loved Ones:** Consider inviting family and friends to join you in the process. This can lead to meaningful conversations about family heirlooms and shared memories.

5. **Practice "Gifting" Instead of Keeping:** View decluttering as an opportunity to gift items to others who will appreciate them, making it feel less like a loss.
6. **Be Selective with Sentimental Items:** It's essential to curate your keepsakes. Take photos of items you're letting go of, create a "memory box," and consider whether future generations would value certain heirlooms.
7. **Enjoy the Process—It Doesn't Have to Be Serious!** While the concept may seem somber, you can make it enjoyable. Set a positive atmosphere, involve a friend for motivation, and celebrate your progress.

Moving Forward: The Start of Something New

Now that you're introduced to the gentle art of Swedish death cleaning, it's time to take that first step. Start small, be intentional, and remember that this journey is about more than just clearing physical space; it's about creating emotional room for what truly matters.

Swedish death cleaning is an ongoing process. Whether you're just starting or already in the midst of decluttering, each small step moves you toward a lighter, freer, and more intentional life.

So grab that cluttered drawer, turn up the music, and embrace the joy of letting go. Swedish death cleaning isn't just about organizing your belongings—it's about creating space to live fully, happily, and with purpose.

Congratulations on beginning your Swedish death cleaning journey! Here's to living light and free.

My Goals For This Week

Date: 7.5.2025

My 3 goals for decluttering this week is... Are

1 My number one goal this week is: Get Rid of 5 Books

I need to take these steps to reach it:
1. Pick the shelf
2. Get a bag
3. Put 5 books in it
4. Bonus if more fit

2 My second goal this week is: Play the piano

I need to take these steps to reach it:
1. AT 9:30 play from F5 by Bach
2. Set timer for 10 min.
3. Find mozart
4. Bonus for more time.

3 My third goal this week is: Drawing one inch gems

I need to take these steps to reach it:
1. Go to art
2. Draw the images. color
3. Cut them out - pack. ADDRess
4. Bonus for more drawings

HABIT TRACKER

Month: _____   Week: _____

HABITS	SUN	MON	TUE	WED	THU	FRI	SAT
_____	☐	☐	☐	☐	☐	☐	☐
_____	☐	☐	☐	☐	☐	☐	☐
_____	☐	☐	☐	☐	☐	☐	☐
_____	☐	☐	☐	☐	☐	☐	☐
_____	☐	☐	☐	☐	☐	☐	☐
_____	☐	☐	☐	☐	☐	☐	☐
_____	☐	☐	☐	☐	☐	☐	☐
_____	☐	☐	☐	☐	☐	☐	☐
_____	☐	☐	☐	☐	☐	☐	☐
_____	☐	☐	☐	☐	☐	☐	☐
_____	☐	☐	☐	☐	☐	☐	☐
_____	☐	☐	☐	☐	☐	☐	☐
_____	☐	☐	☐	☐	☐	☐	☐
_____	☐	☐	☐	☐	☐	☐	☐
_____	☐	☐	☐	☐	☐	☐	☐
_____	☐	☐	☐	☐	☐	☐	☐
_____	☐	☐	☐	☐	☐	☐	☐
_____	☐	☐	☐	☐	☐	☐	☐
_____	☐	☐	☐	☐	☐	☐	☐
_____	☐	☐	☐	☐	☐	☐	☐
_____	☐	☐	☐	☐	☐	☐	☐
_____	☐	☐	☐	☐	☐	☐	☐

What I learned about myself...

What I learned about myself...

CHAPTER 2

Mindfulness and the Decluttering Process

As we explore Swedish death cleaning, it's essential to understand the philosophy guiding this transformative practice. Swedish death cleaning goes beyond merely decluttering your home; it reflects how we approach life, relationships, and the legacies we leave behind. In this chapter, we'll examine the core principles of Swedish death cleaning, its cultural context, and how embracing this philosophy can lead to a more intentional and fulfilling life.

1. The Cultural Context of Swedish Death Cleaning

To fully appreciate Swedish death cleaning, we must consider its cultural origins. In Sweden, a pragmatic approach to life and death influences how people view their belongings and the act of letting go.

- **Acceptance of Mortality:** Swedish culture embraces death as a natural part of life, encouraging individuals to reflect on their lives and the legacy they wish to leave. This acceptance underpins the practice of death cleaning, emphasizing the importance of thoughtful preparation for the future.
- **Pragmatism:** Swedes typically maintain a practical mindset regarding possessions, believing items should serve a purpose. This perspective fosters simplicity and intentional living, enabling individuals to prioritize what truly matters.
- **Community and Connection:** There's a strong sense of community in Sweden, influencing how individuals approach decluttering. Swedish death cleaning encourages people to consider the impact of their belongings on loved ones, making letting go a communal responsibility.

2. The Philosophy of Letting Go

At the heart of Swedish death cleaning is the philosophy of letting go, guided by several key principles:

- **Mindfulness:** Being present in the moment helps individuals reflect on their relationship with their belongings. This awareness allows for intentional decisions about what to keep and what to release.
- **Value-Based Decision-Making:** Letting go involves evaluating possessions based on personal values rather than societal pressures. Focus on whether an item aligns with your values or brings you joy.
- **Emotional Release:** Parting with items often involves emotional release, acknowledging attachments and memories associated with them. Embracing this emotional aspect can lead to personal growth and freedom.
- **Legacy Creation:** Letting go ultimately helps create a legacy that reflects your values and the impact you want to have on others. This perspective encourages thinking beyond your lifetime and considering your influence on future generations.

3. Embracing Minimalism

A crucial element of Swedish death cleaning is embracing minimalism, whose principles align closely with letting go.

- **Simplicity:** Minimalism simplifies life by reducing clutter and distractions, allowing you to focus on what truly matters—relationships, experiences, and personal growth.
- **Quality Over Quantity:** Minimalists prioritize meaningful items that enhance their lives, shifting the focus from accumulating possessions to investing in things that bring joy.
- **Mindful Consumption:** This philosophy encourages critical thinking about purchases. Before acquiring new items, consider their long-term value and alignment with your values.

4. The Benefits of Swedish Death Cleaning

Understanding the philosophy behind Swedish death cleaning reveals its numerous benefits, which can lead to transformative changes in your life:

1. **Emotional Clarity:** Decluttering creates a space for reflection, leading to improved mental health and well-being.
2. **Increased Freedom:** Letting go of possessions allows for new experiences, personal growth, and invigorates your life.
3. **Stronger Relationships:** By prioritizing relationships over possessions, you can strengthen connections with loved ones and create lasting memories.
4. **Reduced Stress:** A clutter-free environment promotes calm and tranquility, enabling focus on what truly matters.
5. **Legacy of Intentional Living:** Your choices about what to keep and let go influence not just your life but also those around you, inspiring a culture of intentional living.

5. Practical Steps to Embrace the Philosophy of Letting Go

Now that we've explored the philosophy, let's put it into practice with some practical steps to help you embrace this philosophy and begin your decluttering journey:

1. **Reflect on Your Values:** Identify what truly matters to you. Write down your core values and use them as a guide throughout the decluttering process.
2. **Set Intentions:** Before you start, establish clear intentions for what you hope to achieve—whether creating a peaceful environment, freeing up space, or reducing stress.
3. **Create a Plan:** Develop a structured decluttering plan outlining specific areas to focus on and a timeline for completing each task.

4. **Start Small:** Begin with manageable tasks, like a single drawer or shelf, to build momentum and gain confidence.
5. **Practice Mindfulness:** Reflect on each item's significance as you sort through your belongings. This mindful approach will help you make intentional decisions.
6. **Be Compassionate with Yourself:** Recognize that letting go can be emotional. Allow yourself to feel sadness, nostalgia, or guilt, and take your time.
7. **Involve Others:** Invite family members or friends to join you in the process. Sharing your intentions and collaborating can create a sense of community and make the journey more enjoyable.
8. **Celebrate Your Progress:** Acknowledge your achievements as you complete decluttering tasks. Celebrating your progress reinforces your commitment to the journey.

6. Moving Forward with Intentional Living

Embracing the philosophy of Swedish death cleaning lays the groundwork for a life filled with intention and purpose. Keep these principles in mind as you move forward:

- **Continuous Reflection:** Regularly assess your belongings, commitments, and relationships to stay aligned with your values.
- **Adaptability:** Stay open to change, recognizing that your approach may need to shift as life evolves.
- **Inspire Others:** Share your journey and inspire others to reflect on their relationships with possessions, fostering positive change.

Celebrating the Journey Ahead

Remember that this process is not linear but a continuous journey requiring patience and self-compassion. Each step toward decluttering offers an opportunity for growth and self-discovery.

Here are a few final thoughts as you embrace the philosophy of Swedish death cleaning:

1. **Cultivate Mindfulness:** Practice mindfulness in all aspects of life, enhancing your overall well-being and making intentional choices.
2. **Nurture Connections:** Prioritize relationships, considering how your possessions affect those around you, enriching your life.
3. **Create Space for Joy:** Let go of unnecessary items to make room for experiences that bring you joy.
4. **Embrace Simplicity:** Simplifying your life allows you to focus on what matters, fostering peace and contentment.
5. **Reflect on Your Legacy:** Your choices today impact your future and those you care about. Reflect on the legacy you wish to leave behind.
6. **Be Open to Change:** Life evolves, and your approach to letting go may need to adapt. Stay flexible and willing to adjust your practices.

Conclusion of Chapter 2

As we conclude this chapter, remember that Swedish death cleaning is a powerful tool for creating a life filled with intention and clarity. By embracing the principles of letting go, you can cultivate a deeper understanding of yourself and your relationships, leading to a more meaningful existence.

In the next chapter, we will delve into practical steps to initiate your decluttering journey, providing you with the tools and strategies needed to start your own Swedish death cleaning process. Together, we'll explore how to approach letting go in a manageable, empowering, and transformative way.

My Goals For This Week

Date: _____

My 3 goals for decluttering this week is...

---

1 **My number one goal this week is:** _____

I need to take these steps to reach it:

1 _____
2 _____
3 _____
4 _____

2 **My second goal this week is:** _____

I need to take these steps to reach it:

1 _____
2 _____
3 _____
4 _____

3 **My third goal this week is:** _____

I need to take these steps to reach it:

1 _____
2 _____
3 _____
4 _____

HABIT TRACKER

Month: _____   Week: _____

HABITS	SUN	MON	TUE	WED	THU	FRI	SAT
_____	☐	☐	☐	☐	☐	☐	☐
_____	☐	☐	☐	☐	☐	☐	☐
_____	☐	☐	☐	☐	☐	☐	☐
_____	☐	☐	☐	☐	☐	☐	☐
_____	☐	☐	☐	☐	☐	☐	☐
_____	☐	☐	☐	☐	☐	☐	☐
_____	☐	☐	☐	☐	☐	☐	☐
_____	☐	☐	☐	☐	☐	☐	☐
_____	☐	☐	☐	☐	☐	☐	☐
_____	☐	☐	☐	☐	☐	☐	☐
_____	☐	☐	☐	☐	☐	☐	☐
_____	☐	☐	☐	☐	☐	☐	☐
_____	☐	☐	☐	☐	☐	☐	☐
_____	☐	☐	☐	☐	☐	☐	☐
_____	☐	☐	☐	☐	☐	☐	☐
_____	☐	☐	☐	☐	☐	☐	☐
_____	☐	☐	☐	☐	☐	☐	☐
_____	☐	☐	☐	☐	☐	☐	☐
_____	☐	☐	☐	☐	☐	☐	☐
_____	☐	☐	☐	☐	☐	☐	☐
_____	☐	☐	☐	☐	☐	☐	☐
_____	☐	☐	☐	☐	☐	☐	☐
_____	☐	☐	☐	☐	☐	☐	☐
_____	☐	☐	☐	☐	☐	☐	☐
_____	☐	☐	☐	☐	☐	☐	☐
_____	☐	☐	☐	☐	☐	☐	☐
_____	☐	☐	☐	☐	☐	☐	☐

What I learned about myself...

What I learned about myself...

CHAPTER 3

Practical Steps for Letting Go

With a solid understanding of the philosophy behind Swedish death cleaning, it's time to dive into the practical aspects of the process. Decluttering and letting go can be emotional and overwhelming, but with a structured approach and the right mindset, you can tackle it effectively. In this chapter, we'll explore actionable steps to kickstart your Swedish death cleaning journey, set realistic goals, and techniques to make the process smoother and more rewarding.

1. Setting the Stage for Success

Before you begin decluttering, it's crucial to prepare both your space and mindset.

- **Establish Your Intentions:** Reflect on why you want to declutter. Are you aiming to create a more peaceful environment, lighten your emotional load, or ease the burden on loved ones? Write down your intentions and keep them visible as reminders throughout the process.
- **Prepare Your Space:** Choose a specific area in your home to start the decluttering. Ensure it is well-lit, comfortable, and free from distractions. Gather necessary supplies, such as boxes for sorting, labels for categorization, and cleaning materials for afterward.
- **Create a Supportive Environment:** Consider inviting a friend or family member for support. Having someone by your side can make the process feel less daunting and more enjoyable. Alternatively, set a peaceful atmosphere with calming music or a lit candle.

2. Understanding the Decluttering Process

To effectively engage in Swedish death cleaning, understand the key steps involved:

- **Step 1: Sort Your Belongings:** Begin by categorizing your items—clothing, books, kitchenware, sentimental items, etc. This visual assessment helps identify areas needing the most attention.
- **Step 2: Use the Four-Box Method:** Label four boxes for sorting:
  - **Keep:** Items you use regularly and value.
  - **Donate:** Items in good condition but no longer useful.
  - **Recycle/Toss:** Broken items or those that cannot be donated.
  - **Sentimental:** Items of emotional significance needing further reflection.

  As you sort, place items in the appropriate boxes to keep the process organized.
- **Step 3: Assess Each Item:** While sorting, ask yourself:
  - When was the last time I used this?
  - Does it bring me joy or serve a purpose?
  - Would I take this if I were to move?

  These questions help clarify what to keep and what to let go of.
- **Step 4: Let Go:** After sorting, it's time to part with the items in the donate and recycle/toss boxes. Schedule a drop-off at a local charity or recycling center. Prompt action is key; the longer items stay in your home, the easier it is to second-guess your decisions.
- **Step 5: Organize What Remains:** After decluttering, organize the items you've chosen to keep. Create designated spaces and consider storage solutions like baskets or bins to maintain order.

3. Starting Small: The Power of Baby Steps

When beginning your decluttering journey, remember that small steps can lead to significant changes.

- **Choose a Small Area:** Start with something manageable, like a drawer or shelf. This approach prevents overwhelm and helps build momentum.

- **Set a Time Limit:** Allocate specific time slots for decluttering sessions, whether 15 minutes or an hour. This keeps you focused and allows for noticeable progress without exhaustion.
- **Celebrate Small Wins:** After each session, acknowledge your progress, whether clearing a drawer or sorting through books. Recognizing these achievements reinforces your commitment to the process.

4. Dealing with Emotional Attachments

Encountering emotional attachments during decluttering is normal. Navigating these feelings is essential for successful letting go.

- **Acknowledge Your Feelings:** Understand it's okay to feel attached to certain belongings. Emotions may arise when sorting items tied to memories or significant events. Allow yourself to experience these feelings without judgment.
- **Reflect on Sentimental Items:** For items with emotional value, consider their significance. Ask yourself why they matter and whether they still serve a purpose in your life. Sometimes, the memory can be cherished without the physical object.
- **Create a Memory Box:** If parting with sentimental items proves difficult, create a designated memory box, limiting its size to keep only the most meaningful items.
- **Practice Gratitude:** As you let go, express gratitude for the role items played in your life. Thank them for the memories they created, helping you release attachments and embrace the space for new experiences.

5. Involving Loved Ones in the Process

Swedish death cleaning can be a shared experience with family and friends, making the process more enjoyable.

- **Communicate Your Intentions:** Share your decluttering goals with family members, explaining your motivations and the benefits. When they understand your intentions, they may support you in the process.
- **Declutter Together:** Organize joint decluttering sessions with loved ones. Working side by side not only makes it enjoyable but also fosters deeper connections through shared stories and memories.
- **Encourage Input:** When sorting shared belongings, invite others' perspectives on what items hold meaning and what can be let go. This creates a sense of unity and shared responsibility in maintaining an organized space.

6. Setting Realistic Goals

Setting achievable goals is essential for staying focused and motivated during decluttering.

- **Break Down Goals into Actionable Steps:** Instead of an overarching goal like "declutter my entire home," break it down into smaller tasks. Aim to declutter one room per week or sort a specific category, like clothing or kitchenware.
- **Be Flexible:** Life is unpredictable, and challenges may disrupt your plans. Be willing to adjust your goals and slow down if needed.
- **Track Your Progress:** Keep a record of your decluttering achievements. Whether through a checklist or journal, tracking progress reflects how far you've come and motivates you to continue.

7. The Emotional Journey of Letting Go

Decluttering is both a physical and emotional process. Understanding this journey is essential for a successful experience.

- **Expect Emotional Ups and Downs:** Prepare for a range of emotions, from excitement and relief to sadness or guilt. Allowing yourself to feel these emotions can facilitate healing.
- **Create Space for Reflection:** After each session, take time to reflect on the emotions that arose. Journaling can help you process feelings and gain insights into your relationship with your belongings.
- **Practice Self-Compassion:** Be kind to yourself throughout the process. Acknowledge that letting go can be challenging and give yourself permission to grieve the loss of certain items. Remember, progress is the goal, not perfection.

8. The Joy of Letting Go

Letting go of excess belongings can be a joyful and liberating experience. Embracing this joy transforms your decluttering journey into an empowering process.

- **Focus on Positive Outcomes:** Shift your mindset to the benefits of decluttering. Visualize the peaceful environment you're creating and the emotional freedom gained. Each item you release makes room for new experiences and opportunities.
- **Celebrate Small Victories:** Acknowledge every step toward decluttering as a victory. After sorting through a challenging area, treat yourself to something small that brings joy—a favorite snack, a relaxing bath, or a leisurely walk outdoors.
- **Engage in Joyful Activities:** As you clear clutter, make time for activities that bring you happiness. Prioritize experiences that enhance your well-being, reinforcing the idea that letting go opens doors to new opportunities.

9. Developing a Sustainable Decluttering Mindset

Creating a clutter-free environment is a lifestyle that requires ongoing commitment. Cultivating a sustainable decluttering mindset helps maintain your progress long-term.

- **Make Decluttering a Regular Practice:** Integrate decluttering into your routine by scheduling regular check-ins. Establish a monthly or seasonal schedule to assess belongings and ensure they align with your values.
- **Cultivate Mindfulness in Daily Life:** Embrace mindfulness not just during decluttering but in your daily consumption habits. Before purchasing new items, ask if they align with your values and will enhance your well-being.
- **Adopt the One-In, One-Out Rule:** To prevent clutter from accumulating, implement the one-in, one-out rule. For every new item you bring home, commit to letting go of an existing one. This reinforces your commitment to maintaining a clutter-free space.

10. Creating a Supportive Environment

To sustain your decluttering efforts, create an environment that supports your goals.

- **Design a Clutter-Free Home:** Arrange your space to promote organization and simplicity. Designate areas for frequently used items, ensuring everything has a home to maintain order.
- **Limit Distractions:** Minimize distractions during decluttering sessions. Turn off phone notifications and find a quiet space to work. A calm environment allows for deeper reflection and more productive decluttering.
- **Seek Inspiration:** Surround yourself with inspirational materials—books on minimalism, decluttering blogs, or online communities

focused on intentional living. Engaging with this content motivates you to stay committed and offers fresh ideas.

11. The Ripple Effect of Letting Go

Recognize that your actions have a ripple effect on those around you. Your commitment to letting go can inspire others to reevaluate their relationships with possessions.

- **Leading by Example:** By embracing Swedish death cleaning, you become a role model. Your willingness to prioritize meaningful experiences encourages others to do the same. Sharing your journey can spark conversations about decluttering and intentional living.
- **Creating a Community of Support:** Connect with others who share your commitment to decluttering. Join local groups or online forums to foster camaraderie as you navigate your journeys together.
- **Fostering a Culture of Letting Go:** Your clutter-free environment contributes to a broader culture of intentional living. Encourage friends and family to embrace similar practices through hosting decluttering events or sharing insights.

Conclusion

In this chapter, we've explored the practical steps to initiate your journey into Swedish death cleaning. From setting intentions and preparing your space to understanding the emotional journey of letting go, each aspect plays a vital role in the decluttering process.

As you move forward, remember that the journey of Swedish death cleaning is deeply personal. Approach it with patience and self-compassion. Embrace the joy of letting go, celebrate your progress, and cultivate a sustainable decluttering mindset.

In the next chapter, we will delve deeper into the emotional aspects of decluttering, exploring how letting go can lead to healing, self-discovery, and personal growth. Together, we will navigate the complexities of attachment, nostalgia, and the freedom that comes from embracing a clutter-free life.

My Goals For This Week

Date: _____

My 3 goals for decluttering this week is...

---

1 | **My number one goal this week is:** _____

I need to take these steps to reach it:

1 _____
2 _____
3 _____
4 _____

2 | **My second goal this week is:** _____

I need to take these steps to reach it:

1 _____
2 _____
3 _____
4 _____

3 | **My third goal this week is:** _____

I need to take these steps to reach it:

1 _____
2 _____
3 _____
4 _____

HABIT TRACKER

Month: _____ Week: _____

HABITS	SUN	MON	TUE	WED	THU	FRI	SAT
_____	☐	☐	☐	☐	☐	☐	☐
_____	☐	☐	☐	☐	☐	☐	☐
_____	☐	☐	☐	☐	☐	☐	☐
_____	☐	☐	☐	☐	☐	☐	☐
_____	☐	☐	☐	☐	☐	☐	☐
_____	☐	☐	☐	☐	☐	☐	☐
_____	☐	☐	☐	☐	☐	☐	☐
_____	☐	☐	☐	☐	☐	☐	☐
_____	☐	☐	☐	☐	☐	☐	☐
_____	☐	☐	☐	☐	☐	☐	☐
_____	☐	☐	☐	☐	☐	☐	☐
_____	☐	☐	☐	☐	☐	☐	☐
_____	☐	☐	☐	☐	☐	☐	☐
_____	☐	☐	☐	☐	☐	☐	☐
_____	☐	☐	☐	☐	☐	☐	☐
_____	☐	☐	☐	☐	☐	☐	☐
_____	☐	☐	☐	☐	☐	☐	☐
_____	☐	☐	☐	☐	☐	☐	☐
_____	☐	☐	☐	☐	☐	☐	☐
_____	☐	☐	☐	☐	☐	☐	☐
_____	☐	☐	☐	☐	☐	☐	☐
_____	☐	☐	☐	☐	☐	☐	☐
_____	☐	☐	☐	☐	☐	☐	☐

What I learned about myself...

What I learned about myself...

CHAPTER 4

The Emotional Journey of Letting Go

Letting go is as much an emotional journey as it is a physical one. While decluttering involves sorting through items and deciding what to keep or discard, the emotional complexities can be overwhelming. In this chapter, we'll explore the emotional journey of letting go, how to navigate the feelings that arise, and practical strategies to support you through this transformative process.

1. Understanding Emotional Attachments

As you begin decluttering, it's important to recognize the emotional attachments you may have to certain items. These attachments can stem from various sources, including memories, relationships, and experiences.

- **Sentimental Value:** Many belongings carry sentimental significance, representing cherished moments in our lives. For instance, a childhood toy may evoke feelings of innocence and joy, while an inherited piece of jewelry may symbolize deep emotional connections. Acknowledging these attachments is crucial as you sort through your belongings.
- **Nostalgia and Memory:** Nostalgia can significantly influence your emotional attachments to items. Certain possessions may remind you of specific times, places, or people, triggering a flood of memories. While these recollections can be comforting, they can also complicate the process of letting go.
- **Guilt and Obligation:** Feelings of guilt or obligation can arise from items received as gifts or inherited from family members. This sense of duty can make it difficult to part with items that no longer hold meaning for you. Recognizing and addressing these emotions is vital for your decluttering journey.

2. The Role of Grief in Letting Go

Letting go of belongings can evoke feelings of grief. This grief encompasses not just the physical items but also the memories and experiences they represent.

- **Creating Rituals for Closure:** Engaging in rituals can provide closure as you let go of belongings. For example, consider writing a letter to an item, expressing gratitude for the memories it holds before parting with it. This acknowledgment can help release your attachment gracefully.
- **Embracing Change:** Understand that change is a natural part of life. By letting go of possessions, you create space for new experiences and opportunities. Accepting the inevitability of change can help you navigate the emotional challenges of decluttering.

3. The Emotional Rollercoaster of Decluttering

Decluttering can be an emotional rollercoaster filled with ups and downs. Understanding this journey can help you approach the process with compassion and patience.

- **Excitement and Motivation:** At the start of your decluttering journey, you may feel excited and motivated to create a clutter-free space. Celebrate this initial momentum as it energizes your efforts.
- **Doubt and Frustration:** As you delve deeper, doubts and frustrations may arise. You might second-guess your decisions or feel overwhelmed by the volume of items. Remind yourself of your intentions and the reasons behind your journey.
- **Joy and Relief:** As you let go of items, you may experience joy and relief. Releasing belongings can lift a weight off your shoulders, creating a sense of lightness. Celebrate these liberating moments as you progress.

- **Sadness and Regret:** It's natural to feel sadness or regret when parting with items that hold significant memories. Allow yourself to experience these emotions fully, practicing self-compassion. Acknowledge that it's okay to feel loss while also reminding yourself of the positive outcomes of letting go.

4. Strategies for Navigating the Emotional Journey

To navigate the emotional complexities of letting go, consider implementing these strategies:

1. **Practice Mindfulness:** Mindfulness helps manage emotions during decluttering by encouraging you to be present and observe your thoughts and feelings without judgment.

    - **Engage in Mindful Breathing:** Take deep breaths before starting each decluttering session to ground yourself. When feeling overwhelmed, pause to breathe deeply, allowing your mind to settle.
    - **Observe Your Emotions:** As you sort items, pay attention to the emotions that arise. Instead of suppressing these feelings, acknowledge them. Keeping a journal to document your emotional responses can also be beneficial.

2. **Create a Support System:** Surrounding yourself with a supportive network can significantly aid your emotional journey.

    - **Involve Friends or Family:** Invite trusted friends or family members to join you during decluttering. Their presence provides emotional support, and discussing your thoughts and feelings fosters connection.
    - **Join Support Groups:** Consider joining support groups or online communities focused on decluttering and minimalism.

Engaging with others who share similar experiences offers validation and inspiration.

3. **Reflect on Your Progress:** Regular reflection can help you process emotions and celebrate your achievements.

    o **Set Aside Time for Reflection:** After each decluttering session, take a moment to reflect on your accomplishments. What emotions arose? What insights did you gain? This practice reinforces your commitment and allows for learning.
    o **Celebrate Milestones:** Acknowledge and celebrate milestones along the way, whether completing a room or parting with a sentimental item. These celebrations remind you of your progress and motivate you to continue.

5. The Freedom of Letting Go

Embracing letting go can lead to profound freedom and liberation. Releasing physical possessions also frees you from emotional burdens that may have held you back.

- **Letting Go of Guilt:** Guilt is a significant emotional barrier to decluttering. You may feel guilty for not using certain items or for parting with gifts. Acknowledge this guilt but prioritize your well-being. Letting go of items that no longer serve you is a healthy choice.
- **Creating Space for New Opportunities:** Decluttering creates physical and emotional space for new experiences. Each item you release opens the door to possibilities, whether pursuing hobbies, spending more time with loved ones, or enjoying a calmer living environment.
- **Embracing Personal Growth:** Letting go fosters personal growth. Confronting attachments and navigating the emotions that arise

leads to insights into your values, priorities, and desires, promoting a deeper understanding of yourself.

6. Moving Forward After Letting Go

After successfully navigating the emotional journey of letting go, consider how to maintain your progress.

1. **Establish New Habits:** Building new habits around your possessions and mindset will help sustain a clutter-free lifestyle.
    - **Daily Decluttering Practices:** Set aside a few minutes daily to tidy up and assess your belongings. This practice prevents clutter from accumulating and reinforces your commitment to intentional living.
    - **Review Your Possessions Regularly:** Schedule regular check-ins to evaluate your belongings, assessing whether they align with your values and adjusting as needed.

2. **Cultivate a Mindful Consumption Mindset:** Embrace a mindful consumption approach to make intentional choices about what you bring into your life.
    - **Pause Before Purchasing:** Implement a waiting period before making new purchases, allowing time to consider whether the item truly adds value.
    - **Focus on Quality Over Quantity:** Invest in quality items that will serve you well over time, prioritizing meaningful possessions that enhance your life.

3. **Share Your Insights with Others:** Your journey of letting go can inspire those around you.
    - **Host Decluttering Gatherings:** Organize gatherings with friends and family to sort through belongings together. This

collaborative approach fosters connection and support while making the process enjoyable.
- o **Engage in Conversations About Minimalism:** Initiate discussions about minimalism and intentional living, sparking interest and motivating others to explore their relationships with clutter.

Conclusion

In this chapter, we explored the emotional journey of letting go, delving into the complexities of attachment, grief, and the freedom that arises from decluttering. Recognizing the emotional aspects of this process is vital for a successful journey.

We discussed various emotional attachments, including sentimental value, nostalgia, and guilt. Acknowledging and processing these emotions is essential for personal growth and well-being. As you navigate the emotional rollercoaster of decluttering, approach yourself with compassion and view the journey as an opportunity for self-discovery.

The strategies outlined—practicing mindfulness, creating a support system, and reflecting on your progress—are essential tools for navigating the emotional landscape of letting go. By implementing these practices, you can foster emotional resilience and make the process more rewarding.

As you embrace the freedom that comes from letting go, consider the positive impact it will have on your life. Each item released creates space for new experiences, opportunities, and connections. Letting go is not merely about clearing physical space; it's about creating a life filled with intention, joy, and meaningful relationships.

Moving Forward with Intention

As you continue your decluttering journey, remember that letting go is an ongoing process. Life is dynamic, and your needs and values may evolve. Embrace these changes and stay open to new possibilities.

The skills you develop through this journey will help you cultivate a more intentional and fulfilling life. By adopting a mindset of mindful consumption and continuous reflection, you can maintain your progress and create a legacy that aligns with your values.

In the next chapter, we'll delve into the practical aspects of Swedish death cleaning, providing actionable steps to implement the principles we've discussed. Together, we will explore tangible strategies to declutter your home and create a space that reflects your newfound clarity and intention.

Additional Reflections

1. **Gratitude for the Journey:** Reflect on your journey of letting go and express gratitude for the experiences and growth that have emerged. Consider keeping a gratitude journal to document the positive changes in your life.
2. **Building a Supportive Community:** Engage with others on similar journeys for invaluable support and encouragement. Connecting with like-minded individuals fosters camaraderie and motivation.
3. **The Importance of Self-Care:** Prioritize self-care throughout the decluttering process. Take breaks and engage in activities that recharge you, such as nature walks or favorite hobbies.
4. **Envisioning Your Future:** As you release possessions, envision the life you want to create. What kind of experiences do you wish to pursue? Letting go opens up possibilities and allows you to align your actions with your aspirations. Dream big and use this journey as a springboard for personal growth.

Final Thoughts

The emotional journey of letting go is a vital aspect of Swedish death cleaning. As you navigate this process, remember to approach yourself with kindness and compassion. Allow yourself to feel the emotions that arise; they are part of the journey. Each step you take toward decluttering is a step toward a lighter, more intentional life.

Embrace the freedom that comes from letting go and celebrate the progress you've made. In the next chapter, we will explore practical strategies for implementing Swedish death cleaning in your home, helping you take actionable steps toward a clutter-free life. Together, we'll delve into how to create a space that reflects your values and aspirations.

My Goals For This Week

Date: _____

My 3 goals for decluttering this week is...

---

1 | **My number one goal this week is:** _____

I need to take these steps to reach it:

1 _____
2 _____
3 _____
4 _____

2 | **My second goal this week is:** _____

I need to take these steps to reach it:

1 _____
2 _____
3 _____
4 _____

3 | **My third goal this week is:** _____

I need to take these steps to reach it:

1 _____
2 _____
3 _____
4 _____

HABIT TRACKER

Month: _____ Week: _____

HABITS	SUN	MON	TUE	WED	THU	FRI	SAT
....	☐	☐	☐	☐	☐	☐	☐
....	☐	☐	☐	☐	☐	☐	☐
....	☐	☐	☐	☐	☐	☐	☐
....	☐	☐	☐	☐	☐	☐	☐
....	☐	☐	☐	☐	☐	☐	☐
....	☐	☐	☐	☐	☐	☐	☐
....	☐	☐	☐	☐	☐	☐	☐
....	☐	☐	☐	☐	☐	☐	☐
....	☐	☐	☐	☐	☐	☐	☐
....	☐	☐	☐	☐	☐	☐	☐
....	☐	☐	☐	☐	☐	☐	☐
....	☐	☐	☐	☐	☐	☐	☐
....	☐	☐	☐	☐	☐	☐	☐
....	☐	☐	☐	☐	☐	☐	☐
....	☐	☐	☐	☐	☐	☐	☐
....	☐	☐	☐	☐	☐	☐	☐
....	☐	☐	☐	☐	☐	☐	☐
....	☐	☐	☐	☐	☐	☐	☐
....	☐	☐	☐	☐	☐	☐	☐
....	☐	☐	☐	☐	☐	☐	☐
....	☐	☐	☐	☐	☐	☐	☐
....	☐	☐	☐	☐	☐	☐	☐

What I learned about myself...

What I learned about myself...

CHAPTER 5

Creating a Supportive Environment for Letting Go

With a solid understanding of the philosophy behind Swedish death cleaning and the emotional journey of letting go, it's time to implement practical steps for the process. This chapter offers actionable strategies to effectively practice Swedish death cleaning in your home. Whether you're just starting your decluttering journey or refining existing practices, these steps will help you create a clutter-free space that aligns with your values and enhances your well-being.

1. Establishing Your Decluttering Goals

Before diving into decluttering, it's vital to establish clear goals that will guide your efforts. Specific intentions will motivate you and help you stay focused throughout the journey.

- **Reflect on Your Intentions:** Spend some time considering why you want to engage in Swedish death cleaning. What do you hope to achieve—whether it's creating a peaceful environment, improving functionality, or preparing for future generations? Write down your intentions and keep them visible as reminders.
- **Set SMART Goals:** Utilize the SMART criteria (Specific, Measurable, Achievable, Relevant, Time-bound) to establish clear decluttering objectives. For example:
  - **Specific:** "I want to declutter my kitchen cabinets."
  - **Measurable:** "I will donate at least five items from the kitchen."
  - **Achievable:** "I can dedicate one hour each Saturday to decluttering."
  - **Relevant:** "This aligns with my intention to create a more organized kitchen."
  - **Time-bound:** "I will complete this task by the end of the month."
- **Visualize Your Ideal Space:** Envision what a clutter-free space looks and feels like to you. Consider how you want your home to function

and the atmosphere you wish to create. Visualizing your ideal space can serve as motivation as you progress through the decluttering process.

2. Choosing the Right Space to Start

Selecting the right area to begin your decluttering journey is crucial for success. Starting with a manageable space helps build momentum and confidence.

- **Begin with a Small Area:** Start with a small space, like a drawer, shelf, or closet. This manageable approach allows you to experience quick wins, which can boost motivation.
- **Assess Shared Spaces:** If you share your living space, consider beginning in shared areas. This promotes collaboration and inclusivity. Discuss your intentions with housemates and invite them to participate in the decluttering process.
- **Create a Decluttering Plan:** Develop a plan outlining the areas to tackle. You might decide to declutter one room at a time or focus on specific categories (e.g., clothing, books, kitchenware). A clear plan keeps you organized and prevents feeling overwhelmed.

3. The Four-Box Method

The four-box method is an effective technique for decluttering that simplifies the sorting process.

1. **Gather Your Supplies:** Collect four boxes or containers and label them:
    - **Keep:** Items you use regularly and value.
    - **Donate:** Good-condition items that no longer serve you.
    - **Recycle/Toss:** Broken items or those that cannot be donated.

- **Sentimental:** Items with emotional significance requiring further reflection.

2. **Sort Your Items:** As you go through your belongings, place each item in one of the boxes. Be honest about what you truly need and value, aiming to create space for what matters most in your life.
3. **Make Decisions Quickly:** Trust your instincts and make swift decisions regarding each item's category. If you hesitate, ask yourself why you're holding onto it and whether it aligns with your values.
4. **Take Action on the Boxes:** Once sorted, it's time to take action:
   - **Keep:** Find a designated, organized space for the items you're keeping.
   - **Donate:** Schedule a time to drop off donations at a local charity.
   - **Recycle/Toss:** Dispose of broken items responsibly.
   - **Sentimental:** Reflect on these items and decide whether to keep them, preserve the memories creatively, or let them go.

4. The Art of Letting Go

Letting go can be challenging, especially with emotional attachments involved. However, embracing this process is essential for successful decluttering.

- **Practice Gratitude:** As you part with items, express gratitude for the roles they played in your life. Thank them for their service and the memories they hold, which can ease the emotional burden of letting go.
- **Recognize Your Attachment:** Understand that emotional attachments are normal. Acknowledge your feelings and allow yourself to grieve the loss of certain items, facilitating personal growth and healing.

- **Visualize Your Space:** As you declutter, picture your home without clutter. Imagine how it will feel and function once unnecessary items are gone. This visualization can motivate you to keep moving forward.
- **Create a "Letting Go" Ritual:** Consider developing a ritual to help with letting go. This might involve writing down your feelings, sharing memories with a friend, or holding a small farewell ceremony for cherished items. Rituals provide closure and aid in navigating emotional challenges.

5. Involving Others in the Process

Swedish death cleaning can be a shared experience that fosters connection and support.

- **Communicate Your Goals:** Share your decluttering objectives with family or housemates. Explain your motivations and invite them to participate. When others understand your intentions, they're more likely to support your efforts.
- **Encourage Input on Shared Items:** In shared spaces, invite others to contribute their perspectives on essential items and what can be let go. This collaborative approach fosters a sense of responsibility and ensures everyone feels heard.

6. Developing a Sustainable Decluttering Mindset

Creating a clutter-free environment is not a one-time event; it requires ongoing commitment and a sustainable mindset.

1. **Practice Regular Maintenance:** Once you've decluttered, establish a routine for maintaining your organized space. Set aside time each month to assess belongings and tidy up. Regular maintenance

prevents clutter accumulation and reinforces your commitment to intentional living.

2. **Adopt the One-In, One-Out Rule:** To prevent new clutter, implement the one-in, one-out rule. For every new item you bring in, let go of an existing one. This practice encourages mindful consumption and helps keep your space clutter-free.

3. **Engage in Mindful Consumption:** Focus on mindful consumption as you continue your journey. Before purchasing new items, ask whether they align with your values and enhance your life. This shift will help you avoid unnecessary clutter in the future.

4. **Cultivate an Attitude of Gratitude:** Embrace gratitude for the space you create. Appreciate the freedom and clarity from living with less, reinforcing your commitment to intentional living.

7. Celebrating Your Progress

Recognizing and celebrating achievements throughout the decluttering process is vital for maintaining motivation and commitment.

- **Acknowledge Milestones:** After completing a decluttering task, take a moment to reflect on your progress. Recognize how far you've come and the positive changes made in your life. This acknowledgment reinforces your commitment to the journey.
- **Reward Yourself:** Treat yourself after reaching a decluttering milestone, whether enjoying a favorite snack, taking a relaxing bath, or indulging in an activity you love. Rewards create positive associations with decluttering and motivate you to continue.
- **Document Your Journey:** Consider keeping a journal to record your decluttering experiences. Write about your feelings, insights, and challenges. This reflective practice can serve as a source of motivation as you navigate the process.

8. The Ripple Effect of Decluttering

As you embrace Swedish death cleaning, recognize that your actions can inspire those around you to reflect on their own relationships with possessions.

- **Lead by Example:** By actively engaging in the Swedish death cleaning process, you become a role model for friends and family. Your actions demonstrate the benefits of living with less and prioritizing what truly matters.
- **Foster Community Conversations:** Initiate discussions about decluttering and minimalism with loved ones. Sharing your insights and positive changes can encourage others to consider the benefits of letting go.
- **Create Supportive Spaces:** Transform shared environments into clutter-free zones. This can inspire others to adopt similar practices and promote a culture of intentional living.

9. Reflecting on Your Journey

As you progress through Swedish death cleaning, take time to reflect on your experiences and growth. Reflection deepens your understanding of yourself and your relationship with belongings.

- **Set Aside Time for Reflection:** After each decluttering session, dedicate time to reflect on accomplishments. Write in a journal about your feelings, challenges, and insights to reinforce your commitment.
- **Explore Personal Growth:** Consider how the process of letting go has impacted your life. What new insights have you gained? Recognizing these reflections enhances self-awareness and encourages ongoing development.

- **Identify Lessons Learned:** Pay attention to lessons throughout your decluttering journey. What have you discovered about your values and priorities? Recognizing these insights allows you to carry them forward into daily life.

10. The Long-Term Benefits of Swedish Death Cleaning

Engaging in Swedish death cleaning is about achieving order; it cultivates a lifestyle prioritizing simplicity and meaningful living. The long-term benefits extend beyond physical decluttering.

- **Emotional Well-Being:** A clutter-free environment enhances emotional health. A peaceful space reduces stress and anxiety, allowing you to focus on what matters. Creating a supportive environment boosts your overall quality of life.
- **Enhanced Relationships:** Intentional living fosters stronger relationships. Prioritizing meaningful connections creates opportunities for deeper conversations and shared experiences, enriching your interactions with loved ones.
- **A Legacy of Simplicity:** Practicing Swedish death cleaning creates a legacy of intentional living that can inspire future generations. Your commitment to letting go sets an example for children, family, and friends.
- **Increased Creativity:** A decluttered space fosters creativity. An organized environment encourages focus on passions and interests, opening new avenues for self-expression.

Conclusion

In this chapter, we explored practical steps for implementing Swedish death cleaning. From establishing decluttering goals and choosing the right starting space to using the four-box method and embracing the art of letting go, each step is crucial for creating a clutter-free environment that reflects your values.

As you continue your decluttering journey, remember that this process is not solely about physical items—it's about embracing a lifestyle of intentionality and simplicity. Each decision contributes to the life you want to create, and every item you release opens up space for new experiences.

In the next chapter, we will delve into the emotional aspects of letting go and how to navigate the complexities that arise during decluttering. Together, we will explore feelings associated with attachment, nostalgia, and grief, as well as practical strategies to support your emotional well-being throughout this transformative journey.

My Goals For This Week

Date: _____

My 3 goals for decluttering this week is...

---

1 | **My number one goal this week is:** _____

I need to take these steps to reach it:

1. _____
2. _____
3. _____
4. _____

2 | **My second goal this week is:** _____

I need to take these steps to reach it:

1. _____
2. _____
3. _____
4. _____

3 | **My third goal this week is:** _____

I need to take these steps to reach it:

1. _____
2. _____
3. _____
4. _____

HABIT TRACKER

Month: _____   Week: _____

HABITS	SUN	MON	TUE	WED	THU	FRI	SAT
_____	☐	☐	☐	☐	☐	☐	☐
_____	☐	☐	☐	☐	☐	☐	☐
_____	☐	☐	☐	☐	☐	☐	☐
_____	☐	☐	☐	☐	☐	☐	☐
_____	☐	☐	☐	☐	☐	☐	☐
_____	☐	☐	☐	☐	☐	☐	☐
_____	☐	☐	☐	☐	☐	☐	☐
_____	☐	☐	☐	☐	☐	☐	☐
_____	☐	☐	☐	☐	☐	☐	☐
_____	☐	☐	☐	☐	☐	☐	☐
_____	☐	☐	☐	☐	☐	☐	☐
_____	☐	☐	☐	☐	☐	☐	☐
_____	☐	☐	☐	☐	☐	☐	☐
_____	☐	☐	☐	☐	☐	☐	☐
_____	☐	☐	☐	☐	☐	☐	☐
_____	☐	☐	☐	☐	☐	☐	☐
_____	☐	☐	☐	☐	☐	☐	☐
_____	☐	☐	☐	☐	☐	☐	☐
_____	☐	☐	☐	☐	☐	☐	☐
_____	☐	☐	☐	☐	☐	☐	☐
_____	☐	☐	☐	☐	☐	☐	☐

What I learned about myself...

What I learned about myself...

CHAPTER 6

Maintaining a Clutter-Free Lifestyle

As you navigate the process of Swedish death cleaning, emotional attachments to belongings often emerge, making it challenging to let go of items with sentimental value. This chapter explores the nature of these attachments, their impact on decluttering, and practical strategies for addressing these feelings. By understanding the emotional complexities of letting go, you can create a more liberating decluttering experience.

1. The Nature of Emotional Attachments

Emotional attachments to belongings can arise from various sources, and understanding these connections is vital for effective decluttering.

- **Memories and Associations:** Many items are linked to specific memories. For example, a gift from a loved one may evoke memories of a special occasion, while a childhood toy might elicit feelings of nostalgia. These associations can create strong ties that make it difficult to part with items, even when they no longer serve a practical purpose.
- **Identity and Self-Expression:** Our belongings often reflect who we are and our experiences. Letting go of possessions can feel like losing a part of ourselves, leading to feelings of loss or fear. Recognizing the role these items play in shaping your identity can help you navigate the emotional landscape of decluttering.
- **Guilt and Obligation:** Feelings of guilt may arise from items received as gifts or passed down through generations. You might feel compelled to keep these items, even if they no longer resonate. Acknowledging these feelings and understanding their origins is crucial for making intentional decisions about what to keep.

2. The Emotional Impact of Decluttering

Decluttering can evoke a wide range of emotions, from excitement to sadness. Understanding this emotional journey is key to overcoming challenges.

- **Anticipation and Excitement:** At the start of your decluttering journey, you may feel excited about creating a more organized space. This enthusiasm can energize your efforts and propel you forward.
- **Doubt and Resistance:** As you delve deeper, feelings of doubt or resistance may surface. You might second-guess your decisions or feel overwhelmed by the number of items. Recognizing that these feelings are normal can help you stay focused on your intentions and the positive outcomes you wish to achieve.
- **Sadness and Grief:** Letting go of sentimental items can trigger sadness. You may mourn the memories associated with certain possessions. Allowing yourself to experience these emotions is essential for healing and personal growth. Acknowledge their significance and give yourself permission to grieve.
- **Relief and Liberation:** As you begin to let go, you may experience relief and liberation. Parting with clutter can create a sense of lightness and freedom, allowing you to enjoy your space more fully. Celebrate these moments of liberation as you progress in your decluttering journey.

3. Strategies for Navigating Emotional Attachments

Implementing practical strategies can help you process your feelings and make intentional decisions about your belongings.

1. **Acknowledge Your Emotions:** Recognizing your emotions is the first step toward navigating the emotional journey of decluttering.

- **Allow Yourself to Feel:** Permit yourself to experience whatever emotions arise. Whether sadness, nostalgia, guilt, or relief, acknowledging these feelings is crucial. Remember, it's okay to feel a range of emotions as you let go of possessions.
- **Journal Your Feelings:** Keep a journal to document your emotions as you declutter. Write about the items you're sorting, the memories they evoke, and how you feel about letting them go. This practice can help you process your emotions and gain insights into your attachments.

2. **Reflect on the Meaning of Each Item:** Take time to consider the significance of each item to gain clarity on what to keep and what to release.

    - **Ask Yourself Questions:** As you sort, reflect on questions like:
        - What memories does this item hold for me?
        - How does this item contribute to my life now?
        - Does it align with my values and aspirations?
    - **Create a Story for Each Item:** For sentimental belongings, consider writing a narrative about their significance. Document the memories and the item's role in your life, honoring those memories without needing to hold onto the physical object.

3. **Practice Gratitude:** Cultivating gratitude can ease the emotional burden of letting go.

    - **Thank Items for Their Service:** Before parting with items, express gratitude for the role they played in your life. Acknowledge the joy they brought you. This practice helps you release attachments with closure and appreciation.
    - **Focus on Positive Outcomes:** Shift your perspective to the positive outcomes of letting go. Visualize the space you are

creating and the freedom gained through decluttering, helping you navigate emotional attachments purposefully.

4. **Create a Memory Box:** If you struggle to part with sentimental items, consider establishing a designated memory box.

    - **Limit the Size of the Box:** Choose a reasonable size to limit the number of items you keep, encouraging selectivity.
    - **Curate Meaningful Items:** Fill the box with items that hold genuine significance and evoke positive memories. This curated collection serves as a tangible representation of cherished memories while allowing you to let go of excess.
    - **Reflect on the Box Regularly:** Revisit your memory box periodically. As you reflect on the items, you may find your emotional attachments change over time, and it's okay to let go of items from the box as clarity grows.

5. **Engage in Rituals for Letting Go:** Creating rituals can provide closure and help navigate the emotional challenges of decluttering.

    - **Host a Farewell Ceremony:** Consider a small ceremony for items you are parting with. Gather friends or family to share stories or memories associated with the belongings. This acknowledgment helps release attachments in a supportive environment.
    - **Write a Goodbye Letter:** For particularly meaningful items, write a letter expressing gratitude and farewell. Describe the memories associated with the item. Reading the letter aloud before letting go can provide emotional closure.
    - **Create a Gratitude Jar:** As you part with items, write down associated memories on slips of paper and place them in a gratitude jar. This practice celebrates the positive aspects of letting go while representing your journey.

4. The Benefits of Letting Go

While navigating emotional attachments can be challenging, the benefits of letting go far outweigh the temporary discomfort. Embracing decluttering opens the door to a life filled with clarity, purpose, and joy.

- **Emotional Freedom:** Letting go of clutter and emotional attachments provides a profound sense of freedom. Releasing physical items also lightens the emotional weight they carry, allowing you to embrace new experiences with an open heart.
- **Improved Mental Clarity:** A clutter-free environment fosters mental clarity. With fewer distractions, you can focus on what truly matters—relationships, hobbies, or personal growth. This clarity enhances your ability to make intentional choices.
- **Stronger Connections:** As you let go of possessions, you create space for deeper connections with loved ones. Prioritizing relationships over material items fosters community and support, enriching your life and those around you.
- **A More Intentional Life:** Letting go aligns with a lifestyle of intentional living. By decluttering and simplifying your space, you create an environment reflecting your values and aspirations, leading to a more fulfilling life.

5. Moving Forward with Grace

Navigating the emotional journey of letting go requires patience, self-compassion, and a willingness to embrace change.

1. **Embrace the Process:** Understand that decluttering is an ongoing journey. Allow yourself grace to revisit areas of your home and reassess belongings over time. As life evolves, so may your relationship with possessions.

2. **Seek Support When Needed:** If struggling with emotional attachments, don't hesitate to seek support from friends, family, or professional organizers. Talking through feelings with someone who understands can offer perspective and encouragement.
3. **Practice Self-Compassion:** Be kind to yourself throughout the process. Acknowledge that letting go can be difficult, and it's okay to feel a range of emotions. Take breaks and don't rush; celebrate your efforts, no matter how small.
4. **Reflect on Your Progress Regularly:** Set aside time to reflect on your decluttering journey. Keep a journal documenting your feelings, insights, and accomplishments, reinforcing your commitment to intentional living.
5. **Embrace Change:** Recognize that letting go is part of life's ebb and flow. Embracing change can lead to personal growth and new opportunities. Releasing what no longer serves you creates space for new experiences and adventures.

6. Final Thoughts on Navigating Emotional Attachments

Navigating emotional attachments during your Swedish death cleaning journey is deeply personal and transformative. By understanding the nature of these attachments and implementing practical strategies, you can approach the process of letting go with grace and intention.

Remember, decluttering is not just about physical items; it's about creating a life filled with clarity, joy, and meaningful connections. Embrace the freedom that comes from releasing what no longer serves you, and celebrate the positive impact on your overall well-being.

Conclusion

In the next chapter, we will explore practical strategies for organizing and maintaining your clutter-free space. Together, we'll delve into techniques for creating an environment that reflects your values and enhances your quality of life. By combining the emotional journey of letting go with practical organization methods, you can cultivate a home that truly supports your aspirations.

My Goals For This Week

Date: _____

My 3 goals for decluttering this week is...

---

1 | **My number one goal this week is:** _____

I need to take these steps to reach it:

1 _____
2 _____
3 _____
4 _____

2 | **My second goal this week is:** _____

I need to take these steps to reach it:

1 _____
2 _____
3 _____
4 _____

3 | **My third goal this week is:** _____

I need to take these steps to reach it:

1 _____
2 _____
3 _____
4 _____

HABIT TRACKER

Month: _____   Week: _____

HABITS	SUN	MON	TUE	WED	THU	FRI	SAT
....	☐	☐	☐	☐	☐	☐	☐
....	☐	☐	☐	☐	☐	☐	☐
....	☐	☐	☐	☐	☐	☐	☐
....	☐	☐	☐	☐	☐	☐	☐
....	☐	☐	☐	☐	☐	☐	☐
....	☐	☐	☐	☐	☐	☐	☐
....	☐	☐	☐	☐	☐	☐	☐
....	☐	☐	☐	☐	☐	☐	☐
....	☐	☐	☐	☐	☐	☐	☐
....	☐	☐	☐	☐	☐	☐	☐
....	☐	☐	☐	☐	☐	☐	☐
....	☐	☐	☐	☐	☐	☐	☐
....	☐	☐	☐	☐	☐	☐	☐
....	☐	☐	☐	☐	☐	☐	☐
....	☐	☐	☐	☐	☐	☐	☐
....	☐	☐	☐	☐	☐	☐	☐
....	☐	☐	☐	☐	☐	☐	☐
....	☐	☐	☐	☐	☐	☐	☐
....	☐	☐	☐	☐	☐	☐	☐
....	☐	☐	☐	☐	☐	☐	☐
....	☐	☐	☐	☐	☐	☐	☐
....	☐	☐	☐	☐	☐	☐	☐
....	☐	☐	☐	☐	☐	☐	☐
....	☐	☐	☐	☐	☐	☐	☐

What I learned about myself...

What I learned about myself...

CHAPTER 7

Embracing Minimalism and Intentional Living

Now that you've explored the emotional journey of letting go and the complexities of emotional attachments, it's time to focus on the practical aspects of Swedish death cleaning. This chapter offers actionable strategies for organizing your belongings, creating a clutter-free environment, and maintaining your newfound clarity. By integrating emotional insights with practical approaches, you can cultivate a home that truly reflects your values and aspirations.

1. Creating a Decluttering Plan

A structured decluttering plan is essential for effective Swedish death cleaning. This plan helps you stay organized, focused, and motivated throughout the process.

- **Set Clear Goals:** Start by defining specific, measurable, and achievable decluttering objectives. Consider what you hope to accomplish—whether it's decluttering your entire home, focusing on a specific room, or reducing items in a particular category. Clear goals will guide your efforts.
- **Break Down Your Goals:** Divide larger goals into smaller, manageable tasks. For instance, if your goal is to declutter the living room, break it into tasks like sorting through books, evaluating decorative items, and organizing electronics. This approach makes the process less overwhelming and allows you to see progress.
- **Create a Timeline:** Establish a timeline for your decluttering plan. Determine how much time you can dedicate each week and set deadlines for completing specific tasks. This structure keeps you accountable and ensures consistent progress.
- **Gather Your Supplies:** Before starting, collect necessary supplies such as boxes or bins for sorting, labels for categorizing items, and cleaning supplies for afterward. Having everything ready streamlines the process and minimizes distractions.

2. The Four-Box Method in Detail

The four-box method is a powerful technique for decluttering. Here's a breakdown of how to implement it effectively:

1. **Gather Your Boxes:** Prepare four labeled boxes or containers:

    - **Keep:** For items you regularly use and value.
    - **Donate:** For items in good condition that no longer serve you.
    - **Recycle/Toss:** For broken items or those that cannot be donated.
    - **Sentimental:** For items with emotional significance needing further reflection.

1. **Start with One Area at a Time:** Focus on a specific area before moving on to the next. Whether it's a room, closet, or drawer, concentrating on one space allows you to see results quickly, boosting motivation.
2. **Sort Each Item:** Place each item in the appropriate box, being honest about what you truly need and value. If uncertain, consider placing it in the "Sentimental" box for further reflection.
3. **Decision-Making Questions:** To aid your decision-making, ask yourself:

    - When was the last time I used this?
    - Does it bring me joy or serve a purpose?
    - Would I purchase it again if I saw it in a store today?

4. These questions help clarify your relationship with each item.
5. **Take Action on the Boxes:** Once sorted, it's time to act:

    - **Keep:** Find a designated space for items you're keeping, ensuring they're organized and easily accessible.
    - **Donate:** Schedule a time to drop off donations at a local charity. Prompt action prevents second-guessing your decisions.

- **Recycle/Toss:** Dispose of broken items responsibly, following local recycling guidelines.
- **Sentimental:** Reflect on the items in this box. Consider how each fits into your life and whether you want to keep it.

3. Organizing What Remains

After decluttering, organizing what remains is essential for functionality and maintaining a clutter-free environment.

- **Designate Specific Spaces:** Assign designated places for each item you've chosen to keep. Create specific areas for categories like kitchen utensils, books, or clothing. This organization prevents clutter accumulation and helps you find items quickly.
- **Utilize Storage Solutions:** Invest in storage solutions that suit your needs. Baskets, bins, shelves, and drawer organizers can keep items tidy and accessible. Label containers for quick identification and efficient organization.
- **Implement a System for Incoming Items:** Develop a strategy for managing incoming items to prevent clutter reaccumulation. Consider the one-in, one-out rule: when you bring in a new item, commit to letting go of an existing one. This practice encourages mindful consumption.
- **Establish a Daily Maintenance Routine:** Dedicate a few minutes each day to maintain your organized space. Tidy up surfaces, return items to their designated places, and assess any new clutter. Regular maintenance helps prevent clutter from creeping back into your life.

4. The Emotional Benefits of Organization

Organizing your space offers emotional benefits that enhance overall well-being.

- **Reduced Stress:** A well-organized environment fosters calm and reduces stress. When everything has a designated place, you can find what you need easily, minimizing frustration and anxiety.
- **Increased Productivity:** An organized space boosts productivity. Easy access to items allows you to accomplish tasks efficiently, positively impacting work and personal projects.
- **Enhanced Clarity and Focus:** Organizing belongings promotes mental clarity. A clutter-free environment allows you to concentrate on what truly matters, enhancing your ability to make intentional choices.
- **A Sense of Accomplishment:** Completing the organization process instills a sense of achievement. As you see your space transformed, take pride in your efforts. This feeling reinforces your commitment to an organized lifestyle.

5. Maintaining Your Clutter-Free Environment

Creating a clutter-free space requires ongoing commitment and mindfulness. Here are strategies for sustaining your organization:

1. **Regularly Assess Your Belongings:** Schedule regular check-ins to evaluate your belongings and ensure they align with your values. This could be monthly or quarterly, allowing you to reassess what you truly need.
2. **Create a Clutter Prevention Plan:** Develop a plan to prevent clutter from reaccumulating. Consider implementing daily or weekly tidying routines and set reminders for regular decluttering sessions.
3. **Practice Mindful Consumption:** Embrace mindful consumption as a lifestyle choice. Before purchasing, assess whether the item aligns with your values and enhances your life. Intentional choices can help prevent clutter buildup.

4. **Involve Others in the Process:** If you share your space, involve others in maintaining organization. Communicate goals and expectations, encouraging a shared commitment to a clutter-free lifestyle.
5. **Celebrate Your Progress:** Acknowledge your achievements as you maintain your organized space. Celebrate milestones, whether completing a room or sustaining organization for a set period. Recognizing progress reinforces your commitment to the journey.

6. Overcoming Challenges in Maintaining Organization

Despite your best efforts, challenges may arise in maintaining organization. Addressing these challenges is essential for long-term success.

- **Dealing with Incoming Clutter:** Life can introduce new clutter, whether gifts or unexpected purchases. Develop strategies to manage incoming items, like the one-in, one-out rule or designating an area for new items until you can assess their value.
- **Managing Changes in Lifestyle:** Your organizational needs may evolve with life changes—new jobs, growing families, or shifting interests. Be prepared to adapt your organization strategies accordingly.
- **Adjust Your Systems:** If current organization systems become ineffective, don't hesitate to adjust. Experiment with storage solutions, rearrange items for better accessibility, or re-evaluate how you categorize belongings. Flexibility in your approach helps maintain an organized environment.
- **Stay Accountable:** If you struggle to maintain organization, consider enlisting a friend or family member for accountability. Share your goals and regularly check in to discuss progress. Having support can provide motivation.

7. Embracing a Minimalist Mindset

A minimalist mindset complements Swedish death cleaning and enhances your journey toward a clutter-free life. Embracing minimalism involves focusing on essentials and prioritizing experiences over possessions.

1. **Shift Your Perspective:** Change how you view material possessions. Recognize that true fulfillment comes from meaningful experiences and connections, allowing you to let go of items without guilt.
2. **Prioritize Experiences:** Invest in experiences rather than physical items. Plan outings with loved ones, explore new hobbies, or travel. These experiences enrich your life and create lasting memories without accumulating more belongings.
3. **Limit Distractions:** Minimize distractions stemming from material possessions. Simplifying your environment leads to greater focus on what truly matters. Consider decluttering digital spaces, such as your email inbox or social media accounts.
4. **Engage in Regular Reflection:** Cultivate the habit of reflecting on your values and priorities. Assess what brings you joy and whether your possessions align with those values. Ongoing reflection encourages mindful decision-making and supports a clutter-free lifestyle.

8. The Ripple Effect of Swedish Death Cleaning

Practicing Swedish death cleaning can create a ripple effect, influencing not only your life but also those around you. Embracing decluttering and intentional living may inspire others to reevaluate their relationships with possessions.

- **Leading by Example:** Actively engaging in Swedish death cleaning sets a powerful example for friends and family. Your commitment to

letting go can encourage others to embark on their own decluttering journeys.
- **Creating a Supportive Community:** Consider forming or joining a community focused on decluttering and minimalism. Engage with those who share similar values and goals. Together, you can exchange tips, provide support, and celebrate successes, fostering accountability.
- **Engaging in Family Discussions:** Encourage open conversations about possessions and the importance of letting go. Involving family members promotes collaboration and shared responsibility for maintaining a clutter-free environment.

9. Reflecting on Your Journey

As you continue your Swedish death cleaning journey, take time to reflect on your progress and insights gained.

- **Document Your Experiences:** Keep a journal to record your thoughts and feelings throughout the decluttering process. Write about challenges, emotions, and lessons learned to gain valuable insights.
- **Set New Goals:** Periodically reassess your goals and intentions. As your life evolves, your relationship with possessions may change. Consider new areas to focus on or adjustments to your decluttering approach.
- **Celebrate Your Achievements:** Acknowledge and celebrate your progress, no matter how small. Recognizing achievements reinforces positive habits and motivates continued efforts.

Conclusion

In this chapter, we explored the practical aspects of Swedish death cleaning, focusing on creating a decluttering plan, implementing the four-box method, organizing what remains, and maintaining your clutter-free environment. By blending emotional awareness with practical strategies, you can cultivate a home that reflects your values and enhances your well-being.

Remember that the journey of Swedish death cleaning is ongoing and requires patience, commitment, and self-compassion. As you navigate the challenges and rewards of decluttering, embrace the freedom and clarity that come from letting go. Celebrate your progress and its positive impact on your life.

In the next chapter, we will delve into strategies for maintaining your organized space and preventing clutter from reaccumulating. Together, we'll explore how to create a sustainable lifestyle that supports your commitment to intentional living and decluttering.

My Goals For This Week

Date: _____

My 3 goals for decluttering this week is...

---

1 | **My number one goal this week is:** _____

I need to take these steps to reach it:

1 _____
2 _____
3 _____
4 _____

2 | **My second goal this week is:** _____

I need to take these steps to reach it:

1 _____
2 _____
3 _____
4 _____

3 | **My third goal this week is:** _____

I need to take these steps to reach it:

1 _____
2 _____
3 _____
4 _____

HABIT TRACKER

Month: _____   Week: _____

HABITS	SUN	MON	TUE	WED	THU	FRI	SAT
_____	☐	☐	☐	☐	☐	☐	☐
_____	☐	☐	☐	☐	☐	☐	☐
_____	☐	☐	☐	☐	☐	☐	☐
_____	☐	☐	☐	☐	☐	☐	☐
_____	☐	☐	☐	☐	☐	☐	☐
_____	☐	☐	☐	☐	☐	☐	☐
_____	☐	☐	☐	☐	☐	☐	☐
_____	☐	☐	☐	☐	☐	☐	☐
_____	☐	☐	☐	☐	☐	☐	☐
_____	☐	☐	☐	☐	☐	☐	☐
_____	☐	☐	☐	☐	☐	☐	☐
_____	☐	☐	☐	☐	☐	☐	☐
_____	☐	☐	☐	☐	☐	☐	☐
_____	☐	☐	☐	☐	☐	☐	☐
_____	☐	☐	☐	☐	☐	☐	☐
_____	☐	☐	☐	☐	☐	☐	☐
_____	☐	☐	☐	☐	☐	☐	☐
_____	☐	☐	☐	☐	☐	☐	☐
_____	☐	☐	☐	☐	☐	☐	☐
_____	☐	☐	☐	☐	☐	☐	☐
_____	☐	☐	☐	☐	☐	☐	☐
_____	☐	☐	☐	☐	☐	☐	☐

What I learned about myself...

What I learned about myself...

CHAPTER 8

The Impact of Decluttering on Mental Health

In a world often driven by consumerism and accumulation, minimalism offers a refreshing alternative. It is not merely about having fewer possessions but a mindset that encourages intentional living, prioritization of experiences, and a focus on what truly matters. In this chapter, we will explore the principles of minimalism, its benefits, and practical strategies for integrating a minimalist lifestyle into your daily routine.

Understanding Minimalism

1. Defining Minimalism

Minimalism is a lifestyle choice characterized by simplicity and intentionality, encouraging individuals to evaluate their possessions, commitments, and priorities for a more meaningful existence.

- **Simplicity:** Minimalism emphasizes removing excess to create space for what truly matters, applying this principle to belongings, schedules, and relationships.
- **Intentionality:** It invites conscious choices about what enters your life, helping you align your actions with your values.

2. The Philosophy Behind Minimalism

Minimalism challenges conventional notions of success and happiness through several key principles.

- **Quality Over Quantity:** Minimalists prioritize investing in meaningful items that enhance their lives rather than accumulating possessions for their own sake.
- **Experiences Over Things:** Research shows that experiences generally yield greater happiness than material possessions, as they foster lasting memories and connections.

- **Mindful Consumption:** Minimalism promotes awareness of the impact of purchases on your life and the environment, leading to more sustainable choices.

The Benefits of Embracing Minimalism

1. Enhanced Mental Clarity

Adopting a minimalist lifestyle can improve mental clarity and focus.

- **Reduced Decision Fatigue:** Fewer possessions and commitments simplify decision-making, allowing you to focus on what truly matters.
- **Improved Concentration:** An organized environment enhances your ability to concentrate and boosts productivity.

2. Increased Freedom and Flexibility

Minimalism provides a sense of freedom that positively impacts your life.

- **Less Stress and Anxiety:** A clutter-free space reduces stress, creating a sense of relief and liberation.
- **Greater Mobility:** Fewer belongings allow for easier adaptation to changes, whether moving or traveling, enhancing your quality of life.

3. Improved Financial Health

Minimalism can have a positive effect on your financial well-being.

- **Reduced Spending:** Mindful spending minimizes impulse purchases, helping you save money for experiences and investments that align with your values.
- **Simplified Finances:** A clutter-free life extends to finances, minimizing expenses and commitments to reduce stress.

4. Stronger Relationships

Minimalism fosters deeper connections by prioritizing meaningful experiences.

- **Quality Time:** Simplifying your schedule allows for more time to nurture relationships, fostering community and belonging.
- **Shared Experiences:** Engaging in activities with loved ones rather than exchanging material gifts creates lasting memories.

Practical Strategies for Embracing Minimalism

1. Assess Your Values and Priorities

Reflect on your values to fully embrace minimalism.

- **Identify What Matters Most:** Consider what brings you joy and fulfillment, focusing on experiences and relationships that are significant.
- **Create a Values List:** Write down your core values to guide decisions on what to keep or let go.

2. Start with a Decluttering Challenge

A decluttering challenge can kickstart your minimalist journey.

- **One-In, One-Out Challenge:** For every new item you acquire, let go of an existing one, reinforcing mindful consumption.
- **30-Day Decluttering Challenge:** Tackle one area or category each day over a month to maintain momentum.

3. Adopt Mindful Consumption Habits

Cultivate habits that align with your values.

- **Pause Before Purchasing:** Implement a 24-hour rule before buying, allowing time to reflect on the necessity and alignment of the item with your values.

- **Focus on Quality:** Prioritize well-made items over cheaper alternatives to reduce clutter and promote sustainability.

4. Create a Minimalist Living Space

Transform your home into a minimalist haven.

- **Simplify Your Decor:** Choose a few meaningful decorative items and consider a neutral color palette to promote tranquility.
- **Incorporate Functional Furniture:** Opt for multi-purpose furniture to reduce clutter while enhancing your living space.

5. Streamline Your Schedule

Minimalism extends to time and commitments.

- **Evaluate Your Commitments:** Reflect on activities that align with your values and let go of those that don't.
- **Prioritize Quality Over Quantity:** Engage in fewer meaningful activities to cultivate deeper connections.

6. Engage in Minimalist Mindset Practices

Cultivating a minimalist mindset enhances your overall experience.

- **Practice Gratitude:** Regularly express gratitude for what you have and the experiences you enjoy, shifting focus from material desires.
- **Embrace Imperfection:** Let go of perfectionism in your home and life, finding joy in the simplicity and uniqueness of your experiences.

The Role of Minimalism in Personal Growth

1. Encouraging Self-Discovery

Minimalism fosters self-reflection and personal growth.

- **Identifying Limiting Beliefs:** Decluttering may uncover beliefs tied to possessions; challenging these can lead to self-discovery and empowerment.
- **Exploring Passions:** Minimalism creates space for pursuing new interests and passions, enhancing personal growth.

2. Fostering Resilience and Adaptability

Minimalism teaches valuable life skills that enhance resilience.

- **Learning to Let Go:** Letting go of possessions fosters resilience and empowers you to navigate life's challenges.
- **Building a Growth Mindset:** Embracing minimalism nurtures a growth mindset, viewing challenges as opportunities for learning.

Minimalism as a Sustainable Lifestyle

1. Environmental Consciousness

A minimalist lifestyle aligns with sustainable living practices.

- **Reducing Waste:** Mindful consumption leads to less waste, contributing to a more sustainable planet.
- **Supporting Ethical Brands:** Choose quality items from responsible companies to minimize your environmental footprint.

2. Creating a Legacy of Simplicity

Embracing minimalism can create a lasting legacy.

- **Inspiring Future Generations:** Your commitment to simplicity can inspire others to reevaluate their relationships with possessions.

- **Passing Down Values:** Focus on sharing values and experiences rather than material possessions, fostering gratitude and mindfulness.

Embracing Minimalism in Everyday Life

1. Integrating Minimalism into Daily Routines

Make minimalism a sustainable lifestyle choice by integrating its principles.

- **Morning Mindfulness:** Start your day with a mindful routine, reflecting on your intentions and setting priorities.
- **Evening Reflection:** Conclude each day with reflection on what went well and how you can continue embracing minimalism.

2. Simplifying Your Digital Life

Minimalism applies to your digital space as well.

- **Declutter Your Digital Space:** Organize digital files, emails, and social media to reduce distractions and enhance productivity.
- **Limit Digital Consumption:** Set boundaries for screen time and prioritize meaningful interactions over mindless scrolling.

3. Creating a Minimalist Kitchen

Adopting minimalism in the kitchen enhances efficiency and enjoyment.

- **Streamline Your Cookware:** Keep only regularly used kitchen tools to reduce clutter and make cooking enjoyable.
- **Organize Your Pantry:** Discard expired items and organize your pantry for easy access to promote healthy eating.

4. Embracing Minimalism in Relationships

Minimalism enhances relationships by encouraging deeper connections.

- **Nurture Meaningful Connections:** Focus on relationships that bring joy and fulfillment, spending time with like-minded individuals.
- **Quality Over Quantity:** Invest in fewer meaningful relationships, engaging in deeper conversations and shared experiences.

Overcoming Challenges in Minimalism

1. Addressing Resistance

Transitioning to minimalism may come with challenges.

- **Confronting Fear of Missing Out:** Recognize that choosing minimalism prioritizes genuine value over excessive possessions.
- **Navigating Emotional Attachments:** Understand it's normal to feel attached to belongings, but practice gratitude as you let go.

2. Cultivating Patience and Perseverance

Minimalism is a journey that requires patience.

- **Set Realistic Expectations:** Minimalism isn't about achieving perfection overnight; set achievable goals for a continuous process.
- **Celebrate Small Victories:** Acknowledge progress, no matter how small, to boost motivation and reinforce commitment.

Conclusion

In this chapter, we explored the principles of minimalism and its profound impact on our lives. Embracing minimalism is about cultivating a mindset of intentional living, prioritizing what truly matters, and enhancing overall well-being.

Understanding the connection between minimalism and mental health allows us to harness its benefits for a fulfilling life. Through practical strategies and a commitment to simplicity, we can navigate the challenges of modern living and embrace a lifestyle reflecting our values.

As you continue your journey toward minimalism, remember that it's a personal path that unfolds at your own pace. Embrace the opportunities for growth and self-discovery that minimalism offers, allowing it to shape your life meaningfully.

In the next chapter, we will explore the concept of legacy, examining how our choices regarding belongings and lifestyle impact future generations.

My Goals For This Week

Date: _____

My 3 goals for decluttering this week is...

---

1 **My number one goal this week is:** _____

I need to take these steps to reach it:

1. _____
2. _____
3. _____
4. _____

2 **My second goal this week is:** _____

I need to take these steps to reach it:

1. _____
2. _____
3. _____
4. _____

3 **My third goal this week is:** _____

I need to take these steps to reach it:

1. _____
2. _____
3. _____
4. _____

HABIT TRACKER

Month: _____   Week: _____

HABITS	SUN	MON	TUE	WED	THU	FRI	SAT
_____	☐	☐	☐	☐	☐	☐	☐
_____	☐	☐	☐	☐	☐	☐	☐
_____	☐	☐	☐	☐	☐	☐	☐
_____	☐	☐	☐	☐	☐	☐	☐
_____	☐	☐	☐	☐	☐	☐	☐
_____	☐	☐	☐	☐	☐	☐	☐
_____	☐	☐	☐	☐	☐	☐	☐
_____	☐	☐	☐	☐	☐	☐	☐
_____	☐	☐	☐	☐	☐	☐	☐
_____	☐	☐	☐	☐	☐	☐	☐
_____	☐	☐	☐	☐	☐	☐	☐
_____	☐	☐	☐	☐	☐	☐	☐
_____	☐	☐	☐	☐	☐	☐	☐
_____	☐	☐	☐	☐	☐	☐	☐
_____	☐	☐	☐	☐	☐	☐	☐
_____	☐	☐	☐	☐	☐	☐	☐
_____	☐	☐	☐	☐	☐	☐	☐
_____	☐	☐	☐	☐	☐	☐	☐
_____	☐	☐	☐	☐	☐	☐	☐
_____	☐	☐	☐	☐	☐	☐	☐
_____	☐	☐	☐	☐	☐	☐	☐
_____	☐	☐	☐	☐	☐	☐	☐
_____	☐	☐	☐	☐	☐	☐	☐

What I learned about myself...

What I learned about myself...

CHAPTER 9

Fostering Connections and Building Meaningful Relationships

As we navigate through life, our choices regarding belongings and lifestyle significantly impact our well-being and the lives of future generations. In this chapter, we will explore the concept of legacy and how the act of letting go shapes the stories we leave behind. We will discuss the importance of intentional living, the influence of our choices on future generations, and practical strategies for creating a meaningful legacy that reflects our values.

Understanding Legacy

1. Defining Legacy

Legacy encompasses the values, beliefs, and lessons we impart to others, extending beyond material possessions to include memories and experiences created throughout our lives.

- **Cultural and Emotional Significance:** Legacies can be cultural, emotional, or practical. They encompass traditions passed down through generations, lessons learned from personal experiences, and the ethos guiding your choices. The values instilled in loved ones will shape their lives and influence their journeys.
- **Lasting Impact:** A well-defined legacy can inspire others to live thoughtfully and intentionally, creating a ripple effect that encourages positive change and fosters a culture of caring.

2. The Role of Intentional Living in Legacy Creation

The choices made today shape the legacy left behind. By living intentionally and making conscious decisions about possessions and actions, you can create a legacy reflecting your values.

- **Conscious Choices:** Every decision, from purchases to interactions, contributes to your legacy. Being mindful of these choices ensures alignment with your values and goals, fostering

deeper connections with your life and the lives of those you impact.
- **Emphasizing Relationships:** A legacy rooted in strong relationships highlights the importance of connection and community. The memories and bonds cultivated with others create a lasting impact beyond material possessions.

The Emotional Aspect of Letting Go

1. Understanding Emotional Attachments

Reflecting on the legacy we leave behind requires understanding our emotional attachments to belongings.

- **Nostalgia and Sentimentality:** Many possessions evoke strong feelings tied to cherished memories. While valid, these emotional connections can hinder the ability to let go. Understanding the reasons behind these attachments is crucial in the letting-go process.
- **Guilt and Obligation:** Gifts or inherited items may create feelings of guilt. You might feel compelled to keep them out of respect for the giver, even if they no longer serve a purpose. Recognizing these feelings allows for compassionate decision-making when letting go.

2. Letting Go with Grace

Navigating the emotional complexities of letting go requires grace and kindness toward yourself.

- **Honoring Memories:** When parting with sentimental items, honor the associated memories. Share stories with loved ones or write about what the item meant to you. This reflection helps release the item while preserving its significance.

- **Practice Self-Compassion:** Allow yourself to experience the emotions that arise during the letting-go process. Feelings of sadness, nostalgia, or guilt are normal. Practicing self-compassion helps acknowledge these emotions without judgment, fostering healing and growth.

The Process of Creating a Legacy

1. Clarifying Your Values

A meaningful legacy begins with understanding your values. Reflecting on what matters most will guide your decisions and actions.

- **Identify Core Values:** Reflect on the principles that guide your life. What qualities do you want to embody? What impact do you wish to have on others? Write down your core values to serve as a reminder during the letting-go process.
- **Align Your Actions with Your Values:** Ensure daily actions reflect your values. When choices align with your beliefs, you create a strong foundation for a meaningful legacy. For example, if family is a core value, prioritize quality time and shared experiences.

2. Sharing Your Story

Your personal experiences are vital to your legacy. Sharing them can inspire and guide those who come after you.

- **Document Your Journey:** Write down your life experiences, lessons learned, and values in a journal, memoir, or letters to future generations. Documenting your journey provides a tangible record for others to reflect upon.
- **Engage in Conversations:** Share your stories with family and friends. These conversations foster deeper connections and

provide valuable insights to others. Encourage loved ones to share their stories, creating a rich tapestry of shared experiences.

3. Establishing Family Traditions

Creating traditions helps instill values and foster enduring connections.

- **Celebrate Together:** Establish annual gatherings that bring family and friends together, such as holiday celebrations or reunions. These traditions create opportunities for bonding and reinforce the importance of connection.
- **Pass Down Rituals:** Create rituals reflecting your values, such as a gratitude ceremony at family dinners or a meaningful toast at gatherings. Rituals provide continuity and connection across generations.

The Gift of Letting Go

1. Giving to Others

Letting go provides a powerful gift to loved ones by sorting through belongings now, ensuring they won't have to do it later.

- **Sparing Their Burden:** Decluttering now relieves your family of the daunting task of sorting through possessions later. You provide them clarity and simplicity during a challenging time.
- **Passing on Meaningful Items:** Instead of leaving your loved ones to decipher value and meaning, take time to pass on significant items. Share the stories behind these belongings to enhance their appreciation.

2. Creating Emotional Freedom

Letting go fosters emotional freedom, allowing you to embrace new opportunities.

- **Release Guilt and Regret:** Decluttering can help you release feelings of guilt associated with items you no longer need, creating space for new experiences and growth.
- **Foster a Sense of Peace:** The act of letting go brings peace and closure, opening you to new possibilities and adventures.

Building a Legacy of Intentional Living

1. Encouraging Generosity and Giving

A legacy of generosity can impact those around you. Model this behavior to cultivate a culture of giving.

- **Volunteer Together:** Engage in community service as a family, fostering empathy and connection. Volunteering strengthens bonds and reinforces the importance of giving back.
- **Share Resources:** Encourage sharing and helping others, whether donating clothes or offering support. Acts of kindness create a positive legacy, instilling the value of generosity.

2. Creating a Meaningful Collection

While decluttering involves letting go, it can also include curating a collection that represents your values and experiences.

- **Select Significant Items:** Choose a few cherished possessions that hold special meaning, such as heirlooms or mementos. This curated collection honors your past while keeping your space organized.
- **Pass Down Your Collection:** Share your collection with loved ones, explaining the significance of each item. This storytelling enriches their connection to the items, creating continuity between generations.

The Long-Term Benefits of Decluttering

1. Inspiring Future Generations

Decluttering can profoundly inspire others. By adopting a clutter-free lifestyle, you set an example for those around you.

- **Demonstrating Value:** Prioritizing intentional living shows the value of simplicity and purpose to your family and friends, motivating them to adopt similar practices.
- **Creating a Culture of Letting Go:** Embracing letting go encourages a culture valuing experiences over possessions, fostering healthier attitudes toward consumerism.

2. Fostering Resilience in Your Legacy

A legacy built on intentional living fosters resilience.

- **Teaching Adaptability:** Modeling adaptability prepares future generations to handle transitions with grace, empowering them to navigate life's challenges positively.
- **Encouraging Critical Thinking:** Teaching loved ones the importance of making intentional choices cultivates critical thinking skills, leading to thoughtful decision-making.

Reflecting on Your Legacy

1. Creating a Legacy Document

Consider documenting your values, beliefs, and life lessons. This document serves as a guide for loved ones, offering insights into your journey.

- **Share Your Wisdom:** Include stories highlighting key moments in your life. This narrative provides valuable lessons for loved ones navigating their paths.

- **Invite Family Input:** Encourage family members to contribute to this document, enriching the narrative with their perspectives.

2. Discussing Legacy with Loved Ones

Engaging in conversations about legacy deepens connections and fosters understanding.

- **Share Your Values:** Discuss your beliefs and the principles guiding your life choices. This dialogue creates a shared understanding of what you hope to pass on.
- **Encourage Family Discussions:** Create opportunities for family conversations about legacy and values, strengthening bonds and sharing stories.

The Legacy of Letting Go

1. Transforming Your Space and Mindset

Letting go of excess possessions creates a physical and mental space reflecting your values.

- **Cultivating a Mindful Environment:** A clutter-free home promotes mindfulness and intentional living, surrounding yourself with what brings joy and serves a purpose.
- **Encouraging Reflection and Growth:** Releasing what no longer serves you creates space for self-reflection and personal growth, leading to a more authentic life.

2. Creating a Legacy of Simplicity

Embracing minimalism allows you to create a legacy that prioritizes simplicity and intentional living.

- **Living Authentically:** Aligning actions with values sets an authentic example for future generations, teaching them the importance of living true to themselves.
- **Promoting Sustainability:** Minimalism encourages responsible living practices, instilling a sense of responsibility toward the planet.

Practical Steps for Building Your Legacy

1. Start Small and Build Momentum

Creating a legacy is a gradual process requiring consistent effort.

- **Focus on One Area:** Begin by tackling one aspect of your life aligned with your values, such as decluttering a specific space or initiating a family tradition.
- **Celebrate Progress:** Acknowledge and celebrate your achievements along the way to reinforce commitment.

2. Engage with Your Community

Building a legacy encompasses your broader community as well.

- **Volunteer and Give Back:** Contribute to organizations that align with your values, modeling the importance of service and compassion for future generations.
- **Share Your Knowledge:** Host workshops or discussions focused on decluttering, minimalism, or intentional living to inspire others.

3. Document Your Legacy Journey

Keep a record of your journey toward creating a meaningful legacy.

- **Create a Legacy Journal:** Write about your thoughts, experiences, and insights related to letting go and embracing minimalism.
- **Include Family Contributions:** Encourage family members to add their perspectives, enriching the narrative.

Conclusion

In this chapter, we explored the concept of legacy and how the act of letting go shapes the stories we leave behind. By embracing intentional living, recognizing the emotional aspects of decluttering, and implementing practical strategies, you can create a meaningful legacy that reflects your values and positively influences future generations.

As you continue your journey of decluttering and minimalism, remember that the choices you make today will impact those who come after you. Embrace the opportunity to inspire, empower, and connect with others as you build a legacy of love, intention, and simplicity.

In the next chapter, we will reflect on your journey of letting go, celebrating the progress you've made and the life you've created.

My Goals For This Week

Date: _____

My 3 goals for decluttering this week is...

---

1 | **My number one goal this week is:** _____

I need to take these steps to reach it:

1. _____
2. _____
3. _____
4. _____

2 | **My second goal this week is:** _____

I need to take these steps to reach it:

1. _____
2. _____
3. _____
4. _____

3 | **My third goal this week is:** _____

I need to take these steps to reach it:

1. _____
2. _____
3. _____
4. _____

HABIT TRACKER

Month: ....   Week: ....

HABITS	SUN	MON	TUE	WED	THU	FRI	SAT
....	☐	☐	☐	☐	☐	☐	☐
....	☐	☐	☐	☐	☐	☐	☐
....	☐	☐	☐	☐	☐	☐	☐
....	☐	☐	☐	☐	☐	☐	☐
....	☐	☐	☐	☐	☐	☐	☐
....	☐	☐	☐	☐	☐	☐	☐
....	☐	☐	☐	☐	☐	☐	☐
....	☐	☐	☐	☐	☐	☐	☐
....	☐	☐	☐	☐	☐	☐	☐
....	☐	☐	☐	☐	☐	☐	☐
....	☐	☐	☐	☐	☐	☐	☐
....	☐	☐	☐	☐	☐	☐	☐
....	☐	☐	☐	☐	☐	☐	☐
....	☐	☐	☐	☐	☐	☐	☐
....	☐	☐	☐	☐	☐	☐	☐
....	☐	☐	☐	☐	☐	☐	☐
....	☐	☐	☐	☐	☐	☐	☐
....	☐	☐	☐	☐	☐	☐	☐
....	☐	☐	☐	☐	☐	☐	☐
....	☐	☐	☐	☐	☐	☐	☐
....	☐	☐	☐	☐	☐	☐	☐
....	☐	☐	☐	☐	☐	☐	☐
....	☐	☐	☐	☐	☐	☐	☐

What I learned about myself...

What I learned about myself...

CHAPTER 10

Creating a Legacy of Intentional Living

As you conclude your journey through decluttering and letting go, it's time to reflect on the legacy you wish to leave behind. The choices you make regarding your belongings, relationships, and overall lifestyle significantly impact not only your life but also the lives of those who follow. In this final chapter, we will explore how to create a legacy that embodies intentional living, the importance of shared values, and how your decisions can inspire future generations.

The Meaning of Legacy

1. Defining Legacy

A legacy encompasses more than material possessions; it embodies the values, beliefs, and lessons imparted to others.

It reflects your impact on family, friends, and community, shaping how they remember you and influencing their lives.

- **Cultural and Emotional Significance:** Legacies can be cultural, emotional, or practical, including traditions passed through generations, personal lessons learned, and the ethos guiding your choices.
- **Lasting Impact:** A well-defined legacy can inspire thoughtful, intentional living, creating a ripple effect that encourages positive change and fosters a culture of care.

2. The Role of Intentional Living in Legacy Creation

Your choices today shape the legacy you leave behind. By living intentionally and making conscious decisions about your belongings and actions, you can create a legacy that aligns with your values.

- **Conscious Choices:** Every decision, from purchases to interactions, contributes to your legacy. Mindfulness ensures that these choices align with your values and goals.

- **Emphasizing Relationships:** A legacy rooted in strong relationships underscores the importance of connection. The memories and bonds you cultivate leave a lasting impact far beyond material possessions.

Practical Steps to Create Your Legacy

1. Clarify Your Values

The first step in creating a meaningful legacy is understanding your values. Reflect on the principles guiding your life and what you want to be remembered for.

- **Reflect on Your Priorities:** Consider your beliefs, passions, and qualities you admire in others. Document your core values to guide your decisions.
- **Align Your Actions with Your Values:** Ensure your daily actions reflect these values. When your choices align with your beliefs, you lay a strong foundation for a meaningful legacy.

2. Share Your Story

Your personal experiences are integral to your legacy. Sharing them can inspire and guide those who come after you.

- **Document Your Journey:** Write down your life experiences, lessons, and values, whether in a journal, memoir, or letters to future generations.
- **Engage in Conversations:** Share your stories with friends, family, and community members. These conversations foster deeper connections and provide valuable insights.

3. Establish Family Traditions

Creating traditions within your family or community instills values and fosters enduring connections.

- **Celebrate Together:** Establish annual gatherings or events that unite family and friends, such as holiday celebrations or game nights.
- **Pass Down Rituals:** Create rituals that reflect your values, like a gratitude ceremony during family dinners, reinforcing togetherness and appreciation.

4. Encourage Generosity and Giving

A legacy of generosity profoundly impacts those around you. Model this behavior to nurture a culture of giving.

- **Volunteer Together:** Engage in community service as a family. Volunteering fosters empathy and connection among participants.
- **Share Resources:** Promote the practice of sharing and helping others, whether through donations or offering support. Acts of kindness create a positive legacy.

5. Create a Meaningful Collection

While decluttering involves letting go, it can also include curating a collection that represents your values and experiences.

- **Select Significant Items:** Choose cherished possessions that hold special meaning, such as heirlooms or travel mementos. This curated collection honors your past while keeping your space organized.
- **Pass Down Your Collection:** Share your collection with loved ones, explaining the significance of each item to enrich their connection.

The Long-Term Benefits of Decluttering

1. Inspiring Future Generations

Decluttering has the power to inspire others. By adopting a clutter-free lifestyle, you set an example for those around you.

- **Demonstrating Value:** Prioritizing intentional living showcases the importance of simplicity and purpose, motivating others to adopt similar practices.
- **Creating a Culture of Letting Go:** Embracing the principles of letting go fosters a culture that values experiences over possessions, promoting healthier attitudes toward consumerism.

2. Fostering Resilience in Your Legacy

A legacy built on intentional living cultivates resilience. The values you instill empower others to navigate challenges and adapt to change.

- **Teaching Adaptability:** By modeling adaptability and the willingness to let go, you prepare future generations to embrace change positively.

Conclusion

As we reach the end of *A Life Unburdened: The Swedish Art of Letting Go*, take a moment to reflect on the transformative journey you've undertaken. Throughout this book, we've explored the profound impact of decluttering, emphasizing that letting go is about more than physical possessions; it encompasses emotional freedom, intentional living, and building meaningful connections.

By embracing Swedish Death Cleaning, you have made significant strides toward creating a legacy that resonates with your values and reflects the life you aspire to lead. Thoughtfully evaluating your belongings, sharing your stories, and nurturing relationships have laid the groundwork for a life that prioritizes experiences over possessions.

As you move forward, keep these key takeaways in mind:

1. **Intentional Living:** Continue making choices that align with your values and embrace the freedom that comes from releasing excess.
2. **Mindfulness:** Practice mindfulness in all aspects of your life, being present, reflecting on decisions, and cultivating awareness.
3. **Building Connections:** Foster joyful, supportive relationships and encourage loved ones to join you on this journey of simplicity and intentionality.
4. **Emotional Liberation:** Understand that letting go can lead to emotional freedom. Release burdens of guilt and obligation, opening yourself to new possibilities.
5. **Creating a Legacy:** Your choices today shape the legacy you leave behind. Approach belongings and relationships with care and intention, ensuring a loving and purposeful impact on future generations.

As you continue this journey, remember you are not alone. Your commitment to decluttering and living intentionally can inspire those around you, creating a ripple effect of positive change in your community and beyond.

Thank you for allowing this book to accompany you on your path to a lighter, more fulfilling life. Embrace the freedom and joy that come from living unburdened, and cultivate a space that reflects the beauty of your journey and the love you wish to share with others.

Here's to a life well-lived—one that celebrates the essence of who you are and the legacy you choose to create.

My Goals For This Week

Date: _____

My 3 goals for decluttering this week is...

---

1 | **My number one goal this week is:** _____

I need to take these steps to reach it:

1 _____
2 _____
3 _____
4 _____

2 | **My second goal this week is:** _____

I need to take these steps to reach it:

1 _____
2 _____
3 _____
4 _____

3 | **My third goal this week is:** _____

I need to take these steps to reach it:

1 _____
2 _____
3 _____
4 _____

HABIT TRACKER

Month: _____   Week: _____

HABITS	SUN	MON	TUE	WED	THU	FRI	SAT
_____	☐	☐	☐	☐	☐	☐	☐
_____	☐	☐	☐	☐	☐	☐	☐
_____	☐	☐	☐	☐	☐	☐	☐
_____	☐	☐	☐	☐	☐	☐	☐
_____	☐	☐	☐	☐	☐	☐	☐
_____	☐	☐	☐	☐	☐	☐	☐
_____	☐	☐	☐	☐	☐	☐	☐
_____	☐	☐	☐	☐	☐	☐	☐
_____	☐	☐	☐	☐	☐	☐	☐
_____	☐	☐	☐	☐	☐	☐	☐
_____	☐	☐	☐	☐	☐	☐	☐
_____	☐	☐	☐	☐	☐	☐	☐
_____	☐	☐	☐	☐	☐	☐	☐
_____	☐	☐	☐	☐	☐	☐	☐
_____	☐	☐	☐	☐	☐	☐	☐
_____	☐	☐	☐	☐	☐	☐	☐
_____	☐	☐	☐	☐	☐	☐	☐
_____	☐	☐	☐	☐	☐	☐	☐
_____	☐	☐	☐	☐	☐	☐	☐
_____	☐	☐	☐	☐	☐	☐	☐
_____	☐	☐	☐	☐	☐	☐	☐
_____	☐	☐	☐	☐	☐	☐	☐
_____	☐	☐	☐	☐	☐	☐	☐
_____	☐	☐	☐	☐	☐	☐	☐
_____	☐	☐	☐	☐	☐	☐	☐
_____	☐	☐	☐	☐	☐	☐	☐

What I learned about myself...

What I learned about myself...

About the Author

Attia Zia is a passionate advocate for intentional living and the art of letting go. With a deep understanding of the emotional complexities involved in decluttering, she has dedicated herself to helping others navigate their journeys toward simplicity and clarity.

Through her experiences assisting her 82-year-old mother in clearing out years of accumulated belongings, Attia recognized the transformative power of decluttering. This personal journey not only provided invaluable insights but also sparked a profound appreciation for the relief that comes from letting go of the past. Whether discarding old papers that no longer serve a purpose or donating clothes and items that once held meaning, Attia finds joy in creating space for the new. Each act of decluttering is a step toward a more mindful existence, where every item retained has a clear purpose and aligns with her values.

As a mother of two sons, Attia understands the challenges of balancing family life while striving to create a harmonious home environment. She enjoys portrait and landscape photography, capturing the beauty of the world around her, as well as graphic design, which allows her to express her creativity and vision. These hobbies not only provide her with a creative outlet but also reflect her belief that clarity in one's physical space leads to clarity in life itself.

Driven by a strong desire for travel, Attia seeks to explore new cultures, landscapes, and experiences, enriching her perspective on life. She believes that a clutter-free life can lead to deeper relationships and greater fulfillment. Through this book, she invites readers to embark on their own journeys of letting go, encouraging them to embrace simplicity and create lasting legacies that reflect their true selves.

When she's not guiding others on their decluttering journeys, Attia enjoys spending quality time with her family, exploring new places, and capturing life's moments through her camera lens. She invites you to join her in celebrating the art of letting go and the possibilities that arise from a life lived intentionally, where each day is an opportunity to shed the unnecessary and embrace what truly matters.

NOTES

NOTES

NOTES

NOTES